THE
OLD GIRLS'
NETWORK

THE
OLD GIRLS'
NETWORK

Insider Advice for Women
Building Businesses in a Man's World

Sharon Whiteley

·····················

Kathy Elliott

·····················

Connie Duckworth

BASIC
BOOKS

A Member of the Perseus Books Group
New York

Printed in the United States of America.

Library of Congress Cataloging-in-Publication Data

The old girls' network : insider advice for women building businesses in a man's world / Sharon Whiteley . . . [et al.].
    p. cm.
  ISBN 0-7382-0806-X
  1. Women-owned business enterprises. 2. Businesswomen. I. Whiteley, Sharon.

HD2341.O426 2003
658.4'21'082—dc21

2003011635

Basic Books is a member of the Perseus Books Group
Text design by Brent Wilcox
Set in 11-point Sabon

Visit us on the World Wide Web at http://www.perseusbooks.com

Basic books are available at special discounts for bulk purchases in the U.S. by corporations, institutions, and other organizations. For more information, please contact the Special Markets Department at the Perseus Books Group, 11 Cambridge Center, Cambridge, MA 02142, or call (617) 252–5298.

To our families and dear friends whose love and unconditional support helps fuel our passions in life:

to Richard for your unconditional love and support, to Sheila my mirror and Terry and Henry for my life.

    —SHARON

to Ann, my mother Peg, Margaret, Mary and Bob.

    —KATHY

to my girls, Elizabeth and Caroline, and my boys, Andrew, William, and Tom.

    —CONNIE

CONTENTS

A Business of One's Own

SETTING THE STAGE

A ship in port is safe, but that is not what ships are built for. Sail out to sea and do new things.

Admiral Grace Hooper

It was called the "Breakfast for Champions," the annual fundraiser to benefit the Commonwealth Institute, a non-profit organization that helps women develop entrepreneurial skills and expertise. On this particular June morning in 2001, more than 1,000 women gathered in the grand ballroom of Boston's Fairmont Copley Hotel to network and to honor women entrepreneurs.

Virtually the entire "who's who" of the women's business community was there, as well as investors, lawyers, and others who work with and support women-led businesses. And there was a contingent of aspiring entrepreneurs, eager to make new contacts and expand their networks or to meet potential investors for their enterprises. As the program ended, people left their tables and collected in loose, swirling groups: greeting old friends, making new ones.

We were just getting up from our table. Individually, we each have successful track records as top executives working in finance, consumer marketing, and manufacturing. Collectively, we call ourselves 8 Wings Enterprises, angel investors with a simple mission: to connect women with the resources they need to start and build sustainable, high-growth businesses.

Although hailing from different arenas, we nonetheless shared a strikingly similar perspective on the issues women face in building businesses. We were drawn together by our common desire to help clear the path for women in the entrepreneurial world. We were receptive to the young would-be entrepreneurs who approached us, their eyes gleaming with passion for their business ideas. So when Kate came over to pitch her idea, we gave her our full attention.

Kate had her "elevator pitch," the thirty-second synopsis of her business idea, down pat. Her voice rose for the finale that she was sure would wow us: "And we have no competition." We could tell from the look on Kate's face that she believed she'd clinched our interest with this last triumphant note, but actually the four of us were thinking, "Uh-oh, another 'babe-in-the-woods,' one more newly minted entrepreneur who thinks she has no competition." Kate had made a common mistake because she had never started a business before. She lacked the experience and the "know-how" to go about it as well as knowledge of the ground rules for speaking with investors.

Because we had often discussed the knowledge gap that women face when starting their own businesses, Kate's wrong turn led us to a spontaneously combustible idea.

Sharon watched as Kate disappeared into the crowd: "That's it. We're writing a book."

We speak from experience. Every year, in our role as investors, advisors, board members, and operators, we see hundreds of bright-eyed entrepreneurs pitch business plans to angel investors and venture capitalists, potential benefactors sitting at the big table behind their mountain of gold. And every year that gold is parceled out to the fortunate few.

Here's something that may surprise you:

On average, *95 percent of all investor financing goes to men.*

Why is it that more men get the financial backing to open offices, stock warehouses, and go public, while most women max out their credit cards, borrow from friends and family, and pretty much go it alone? No one has ever seriously suggested that there's a qualitative difference between male and female ideas. We can state absolutely that the marketplace doesn't care who wore pink booties and who wore blue. The marketplace cares only about supply and demand, goods and services.

Is testosterone a better business tool than estrogen? Is it true that women can't take the heat and should stay in the kitchen? The sound you hear is 6 million businesswomen laughing. Or, as a pioneering venture capitalist once said as she took the podium to receive an industry award, "Does this microphone work for women, too?"

FACT: Women's businesses today generate more than half the private sector output of our gross domestic product.

FACT: Women-owned businesses employ more people than the Fortune 500 companies combined.

FACT: Women who start businesses have the same motivation as men: self-actualization, personal achievement, and autonomy.

So why is there a need for a book by women for women?

Because there is a double standard. *Because* we are still laboring under marketplace inequality. *Because* of our cultural, societal upbringing, we still don't feel entitled to succeed, to compete and win. *Because* we don't have equal access to capital.

Because we thrive when someone offers us guidance that helps us move our businesses forward, instead of dismissing us, stopping us in our tracks. *Because* there is a misconception that women don't have the characteristics needed to run an enterprise—the passion, the vision, the inherent skill set.

We've written *The Old Girls' Network* because we know what it's like to hand-feed a tender young business twenty-four hours a day. We've been there. We're there now: piloting companies, coaching other businesswomen, investing in women's businesses. The entrepreneurs we profile in the book are women we know, and many of them we have helped directly by coaching, advising, and, sometimes, investing directly in their businesses.

We believe that the road to equality in every field springs from the practical reality of economic independence. We would argue that collectively women are far less powerful than men, a situation that stems in part from how we deal with money, how we earn money, and how we think about money. We see the disparity in all aspects of life, but especially in business.

This inequity is one of the reasons we encourage those who yearn to create their own businesses but have no role models. We are passionate about helping other women use business as a vehicle to achieve self-actualization and economic independence. We are committed to indomitable dreamers, to women like you.

When asked whether they have a dream, most women say, "No, I'm lucky if I can make it through the day, let alone have a dream." But we do indeed have dreams. Dreams of starting businesses—a bookstore, a marketing agency, the next eBay. We dream of launching a computer software company or of developing a better way to store X-ray images.

Not many of us were told, let alone encouraged, that we could express ourselves through the medium of business. We were not told that by creating and selling products and services we could manifest our ingenuity, our intelligence, our independence; that we could do good for others and have a fully realized life.

Women's dreams are often about the kind of person we want to be or the kind of impact we want to have on the world. It's important for us to realize that business is a diverse and powerful vehicle for achieving these dreams.

All four of us have had profound and enriching experiences in the business world. None of us had ever dreamed of becoming a CEO; rather, we wanted to realize a vision of who and what we wanted to be, and business became our vehicle to that realization.

Along the way, we saw how hard it was for women to convert their entrepreneurial spirit into the reality of a business. We saw that when women succeed, they attribute their success to luck. Yet when they fail, they place the blame squarely on themselves. We saw that women were lacking mentors and role models, a deficit that was a serious shortfall because encouragement pries women out of that fetal tuck and nudges them into tomorrow's challenges. We found that the lack of financial backing put good ideas and smart women out of business before they ever really started—and that a healthy infusion of cash can propel a burgeoning company over the shifting ground of today's financial times.

We also saw that women have traits that help us succeed; our ability to network is probably hardwired into our DNA, as are empathy and intuition, interpersonal qualities that lubricate the business of business. In the course of our combined years in commercial pursuits, we've recognized that the characteristics critical for business success are truly gender-neutral. Those who succeed figure out how to connect their passion to a business idea; they have ironclad determination, what we call "positive perseverance." They are flexible enough to accept criticism, re-think, reverse, re-create, and start again. They have people skills; they can work with others and they can inspire and lead a team.

And successful business people are not only smart; they are tuned in to what's hot and what's not, alert to the vagaries of the marketplace so that they can hone the point of a fundamentally sound business idea.

. . . .

So why the title, *The Old Girls' Network: Insider Advice for Women Building Businesses in a Man's World*? We were famil-iar with the the Old Boys' Network—the invisible club that helps men to advance in the business world by way of their con-nections. What first came to mind was a fun play on words and a way of illustrating a counterpoint to that well-understood and sometimes envied Old Boys' Network. Then we began to reflect on the immutable connection between women and networks throughout history. And we knew we were on to something.

For women, networks are and always have been about build-ing relationships. We are pros at it. Women's ability to forge communities and make connections is ancient . . . it is tribal, it *is* wired into our DNA. It is one of the greatest strengths we have and one of our most critical assets as aspiring entrepreneurs.

While Sharon's declaration was still hanging in the air, we en-visioned a code book, a field guide to help brave, smart, for-ward-thinking women like Kate shorten and enhance their chal-lenging journey toward entrepreneurship. We thought that if we could map the terrain, these women would have a straighter shot at success.

And that would benefit us all.

During the next eighteen months, we put down our thoughts about the traits and skills that turn a business dreamer into a seasoned entrepreneur. We asked a myriad of successful businesswomen to share their personal stories about the roller coaster ride of good times, as well as the near disasters that characterized their paths to the top. That we often learn the most from our mistakes may be a cliché, but it's true. We think you'll find the accounts of these women enlightening, inspirational, and instructive. So know that with this book you have tapped into a deep and valued wisdom base, not just that of 8Wings, but of all the successful entrepreneurs who make these chapters come alive, women who wanted to add their voices to ours.

As we talked to these women about their experiences, we were again struck by how important relationship building is to the whole process of starting, funding, and growing a company. And the value of relationships is a thread that runs through every entrepreneur's story in this book.

From these stories, the book's framework fell into place. Chapters 2 through 5 discuss the key traits all entrepreneurs share—essential must-have qualities without which your business will never get off the ground. There is *passion*, the energy source necessary to push your entrepreneurial dream out of the starting blocks. There is *vision*, which means not only seeing the big picture but also communicating it to enlist the support of others. A *pioneering spirit* embodies intellectual curiosity and a drive to succeed that sets successful entrepreneurs, and all visionaries, apart from the also-rans. And an often-overlooked quality is *tenacity,* the intangible "vapor" you thrive on when your emotional fuel tank runs dry.

Chapters 6 and 7 deal with the more concrete aspects of entrepreneurship: how to raise capital to start and grow your business, and how to stay focused while adapting your business model to changing environments. The last two chapters, 8 and 9, bring it all together by discussing leadership and exploring the challenges and opportunities you face as your business grows.

Within each chapter you'll find expanded definitions of the important concepts introduced; these are titled "Digging Deeper." At the end of every chapter you'll find a recap of key points under the heading "What You Need to Know." The back of the book contains a "Tool Kit" containing templates, sample documents, and other useful information designed to help you apply and tailor the book's concepts to your unique business situation. We've compiled a list of resources, too, including business organizations and Web sites that can help you on your way. Our hope is that this book will illuminate the unnecessarily arcane path to starting and growing a business.

Even with the right skills and tools, it's essential to have a mentor to provide feedback and encouragement as you go forward. If you can't find such a person, or until such time as you do, we hope this book will serve as a virtual mentor. We hope you'll think of us as part of *your network*—your personal coach *and* cheering section, and for those times when it's necessary, your personal butt kicker—and that you'll feel our support as you launch *your* entrepreneurial dream.

We want you to enjoy the business of becoming an entrepreneur. And we want you to win at it, too. Remember, you are not alone. We wrote this book for you.

Passion

TURNING WHAT YOU LOVE
INTO A REAL BUSINESS

*The future belongs to those who believe in the beauty
of their dreams.*

Eleanor Roosevelt

The starting point behind every business idea is passion. For
the entrepreneur, passion is the urge or compulsion to express your creativity by bringing something new into the world—
something that you have daydreamed about for many years,
something—a hobby or a vocation—that excites and energizes
you to the core. You can't learn it. You can't buy it. You know
it when you have it.

. . . .

We believe that if you have a recurring daydream about building
a business out of something you truly love, go for it. Cheryl
Straughter did just that. The last time we saw Cheryl, restauran-
teur and entrepreneur, she was making a presentation to a large
group of business executives, aspiring entrepreneurs, and the

press. From the moment she took the stage, Cheryl was like a sparkler on the Fourth of July. And when she told her story, she just about burned the place down. Her energy was all the more amazing to us when later we found out that she'd been up until 4:30 that morning prepping to cater a luncheon for five hundred people that very day.

Cheryl's story is an example of passion writ large. From the time she was a teenager, she had dreamed of owning her own restaurant—her own place. "In the traditional black family, a lot of activity centers around food and the kitchen. As we were growing up, we would gather in the kitchen because that's where my mother and grandmother were cooking." And this was where the seeds of her passion for starting a restaurant were sown; this was where she found the desire to create a sense of community around good home cooking, not a burger joint or a high-end place. Rather, she wanted to create a neighborhood restaurant that welcomed its patrons as family and was affordable for the average person to visit every day.

A single mother raising her young son, Keith, Cheryl didn't have resources to call upon—no house to mortgage, no collateral of any sort. She soon discovered that passion was her biggest asset: "The part of my presentation that really caught people's eyes was my desire, my drive, and my burning motivation."

As Cheryl illustrates, passion fuels every business idea. The hallmarks of passion are total absorption, round-the-clock engagement, unfiltered imagination, unbridled possibility, and intense motivation. Passion flows from your core. It is your inner flame. What does passion have to do with building a business? EVERYTHING!

Entrepreneurs can be passionate about anything. They can be passionate about galvanized garbage cans, about diesel truck parts, about silk scarves, even about insurance policies. The key is to find what makes your heart sing. Passion is the energy source driving you to create and build your enterprise with an unrelenting focus on your dream. It is the required emotional asset that never shows up on your balance sheet. Jaimee Wolf lives this point fully.

Even as a young girl, Jaimee knew she was destined to become an entrepreneur; while her friends engaged in other activities, Jaimee always played "owner of something." She had her share of lemonade stands and was always conjuring up new business ideas—such as the one where she "borrowed" newspapers from the corner bin and sold them herself. Until, that is, her mom gave her a fast course in business ethics. After graduating from college and becoming involved in several marginally successful businesses, Jaimee found her way back to the one thing that had consumed her as a kid: video games.

Jaimee's interest was first sparked in grade school with Pong, one of the original video game releases. By high school, she had developed a full-blown passion. She perfected her gaming skills while laid low for a month with mononucleosis and then became a fanatic. After a brief foray into the record industry after college, Jaimee found herself in the computer software field; but she still spent her free time playing video games. Finally, she got it . . . what she had learned about producing records and computer software could be applied to licensing and producing video games. There, right before her nimble fingers, was her future. Jaimee had made the connection between her life-long passion and a profitable business opportunity.

Today, her successful global company, Xicat, which publishes video games, is considering filing with the SEC for a public stock offering. With titles such as X-Plane, ChargeNBlast, and Iron Aces, it's this gaming girl's dream come true.

Marcia Weider believes that most passions can be turned into a business, and she has done just that. Now a motivational speaker and the author of *Making Your Dreams Come True*, Marcia has taken the concept of helping others to find their passion and follow their dreams and has built it into a thriving business, Marcia Weider Enterprises. Her clients include corporations and organizations all over the world from the Gap to the Girls Scouts. But it wasn't always so.

Early in her career, Marcia had built a multimillion-dollar marketing and media company. Then, just when the business was running smoothly, suddenly she lost everything. Unbeknownst to Marcia, her bookkeeper, out of negligence and not intent, had failed to withhold payroll taxes and did not make the required payments to the IRS. When the error was discovered, the late interest charges and significant penalty payments that had accumulated forced Marcia to use her company's profits and take a second mortgage on her house to satisfy these obligations. Still it was not enough. "I worked my tail off to pay this debt, but it wiped me out financially. I had been president of the National Association of Women Business Owners, driving around Washington, D.C., in a Jaguar, lunches at the press club, lah-de-dah, and that whole identity collapsed." After a year-long self-described "lost" period and still in transition, Marcia moved to San Francisco, rented a small apartment, and began the process of starting over. "I went from being clear, intentional, and results-oriented to not knowing. And there was something about being in the 'not knowing' that invited a deeper exploration. The promise I made to myself was that I wouldn't go start another business just to be successful. I knew how to do that, but it didn't really feel like that's where my growth was. I wondered what my deeper calling in life would be. This led me to talking to people about purpose and about their passions, which then led me to this new work that I do."

Marcia's passion for starting her new business was ignited while she was volunteering at the Make-A-Wish Foundation, a group that grants wishes to critically and terminally ill children. "I was so moved by who they were and what they were about that I decided that I wanted to make my life about how people can realize their dreams. For me, it wasn't just about sick children, it was about sick companies—organizations where people had lost their vision, lost their passion, and weren't aligned around anything. I think purpose often has to do with mission . . . it's all tied together—purpose, mission, and the passion for what you're doing and for who you're being."

Maxine Clark, CEO of Build-A-Bear Workshops, couldn't agree more. We traveled in her wake as she arrived at the Paramus Mall in New Jersey to open a new Build-A-Bear Workshop, her eightieth in five years. Maxine, a blur of action in her Build-A-Bear uniform of khakis, denim shirt, and red sweater vest with company logo, snipped the red ribbon and hoards of shoppers streamed in. Maxine had trouble describing the delight she felt then: "When I smile, it's such a different feeling. I can't even explain it . . . I wish I could articulate it. I've created an environment where I can be me and where others can be who they are—a warm and fuzzy environment, literally and figuratively."

Maxine began her journey to Chief Executive Bear when she was growing up in Florida. She told us that "shopping was entertainment, engaging and magical." As a young girl in the 1950s, she would dress up and take the bus with her mother to go window-shopping in downtown Miami. "We couldn't necessarily afford what we saw in the windows, but that didn't make it any less fun to go and see and wish. It was pure fantasy with fashion shows, lunch with kiddie cocktails in the tearoom, and white gloves. We especially loved shoes. My mother could stitch up clothes much like the store versions and with the money we saved, we could buy the right shoes and take them home that day."

After college, Maxine headed straight for May Department Stores to indulge her passion for creative retailing; she worked hard to learn every aspect of the business. Twenty-five years later to the day, Maxine became the president of a May subsidiary, Pay-Less Shoe Stores. "I loved my job. Pay-Less was the May Company's largest division, a $2.5-billion, 4,500-store chain. But a day came when I noticed that shopping as a form of entertainment had disappeared, and on a personal level, my own enthusiasm for shopping had crashed. Work, too, was losing its buzz. My psychic income bank account was at zero because I wasn't loving my work any more. I saw that too much of my creativity and talent was being lost to meetings and paperwork. I wasn't having fun."

Maxine toyed with ideas about what to do next, about how to turn the clock back and re-create the excitement of shopping she had felt as a child. In 1996, while touring a stuffed-animal factory, the Build-A-Bear concept hit her. "The idea for Build-A-Bear Workshops was really very much an extension of what I'd done my entire life. When I envisioned the idea, I crossed from corporate businessperson to entrepreneur." She also knew firsthand the power teddy bears have over children. When Maxine was ten, her father took her well-worn "Teddy" away because he thought it would solve her thumb-sucking problem. "It didn't, and I've been looking for him ever since."

In just five years, Maxine has accomplished the unheard of in today's retail climate—the building of an award-winning chain of 113 stores with sales of $170 million, not to mention thousands of satisfied customers and . . . happy bears. "I left the corporate world to bring theater back into retailing and to give back to the industry that had been so good to me. . . . It's all my dreams rolled into one."

So how important is passion? We say it's critical. For a long time when you're taking your vision forward, passion is everything and you are the flag bearer, the embodiment of your idea. Your passion for your business will inevitably go through cycles of "in love" and "in the doldrums," but if you lose your passion altogether, you'll lose sight of the finish line as well. This can spell the end of the race because there's no one else to say, "Oh, come on, you can do it," or "It's a great idea. The world needs you." That's the job of your passion. Cheryl's passion for her restaurant concept drove her to visit every bank in the city of Boston; after being turned down by one after the other, she forged ahead and uncovered a city-sponsored loan program designed to help revitalize the inner city.

Viewed from the outside, passion is expressed by different people in different ways. Some entrepreneurs make sparks fly whenever they're around. For others, the feeling is private, but it burns inside like a bright blue flame. However it is expressed, passion is an energy source that drives you to create and build your enterprise with an unrelenting focus on your dream. It compels you to take risks, to commit to your vision in the face of resistance, other people's doubts, and your own fear of failure.

Passion can't be faked. When you're in love with your business idea, people know it, and when you're acting, they know that, too. Passion is like a magnetic force that gets other people to join your cause without your even asking. It's an energy-to-energy connection: a subliminal suggestion that makes others think, "Wow, this person's going places and doing really interesting stuff and I want to help her."

Bottom line: Passion is the required emotional asset that doesn't show up on your balance sheet, but can stop your business cold if you don't have it.

DIGGING DEEPER

Now that your passion's ignited and you want to get started, you probably don't know where to begin. Here's our list of some of the first things you should tackle:

1. Begin to flesh out your business plan, starting with your vision for the business. The next chapter will assist you in this.
2. Find that mentor who can help you move forward. Start by making a list of the qualities such a person should have and note who in your network could either be your mentor or help you to find that person.
3. Join a local or regional business organization that dedicates itself to developing entrepreneurs.
4. Name your company. Apply for a registered trademark for use in your industry. This will also inform you whether the name is available. If not, get another name. You can begin some of this research on your own on the Internet.
5. Secure your Internet domain name(s) in all venues relevant to your business (".com" usually suffices for commercial ventures). If possible, secure other names similar to the one you will be using, as well as common misspellings.
6. Set up your personal e-mail address under the company domain.

(continues)

7. Design a logo or typeface, create stationery, and have business cards printed. Inexpensive computer-generated materials will suffice early on. Looking professional is important right from the start.

8. Open a bank account—network among your peers to find the bank in your area that is most friendly to small businesses. Explore with them how you can develop a credit history and establish a credit line.

9. Begin to think about your "elevator pitch," a thirty-second synopsis of what your business is and its value proposition. (This is discussed in more detail in Chapter 3.)

10. Decide on the legal form of ownership according to your objectives for the business. If you plan to raise outside equity, most investors will require that your company be set up as a "C" corporation (an industry standard), and also as a Delaware Corporation because of the ease of filing registration documents and its lower cost. (See page 175 in the Tool Kit for a brief explanation of the legal entities and how to decide among them.)

At this stage, it's critical for you to distinguish between a dream and a fantasy. With a dream, you can design a strategy for getting there. A fantasy is more like winning the lottery—there's nothing you can do to make it happen. Are you curious about whether your own passion can be transformed into a business? Or are you saying to yourself that what you love is too small,

Can you turn your passion into a business? See Exercise #1 in the Took Kit, page 176.

too insignificant, or too difficult to translate into the mold of a business entity? If you would like to explore how you can take your passion to the next level, we have included an exercise in the Tool Kit that will help you visualize this transformation.

. . . .

In the next chapter, we discuss *Vision,* another intangible quality embodied in successful entrepreneurs. You need to have a strong sense of your vision and the ability to articulate it if you are to bring your passion forward into a business reality.

WHAT YOU NEED TO KNOW

- Successful businesses often spring from a life-long interest, hobby, or strength from which you now want to make a living.
- Distinguish between an actionable dream and a fleeting fantasy.
- There are many ways to translate your passion into an idea for a business. If your passion doesn't appear at first to lend itself to a business, don't give up. Focus on the source of your passion and look for the multiple pathways to turn it into an enterprise.
- You must be passionate in order to have the stamina to build a business. Turning this passion into a business, particularly in the early going, requires an all-consuming focus—long hours and full-fledged commitment to the effort.
- Being an entrepreneur gives you the freedom to build a business around your vision and values. However, if you think that by being your own boss you'll have complete control of your own agenda, calendar, and time, think again. You have just signed up to serve multiple masters—vendors, customers, investors, employees—who will be clamoring for your time, attention, and resources.

- Passion has a natural ebb and flow. Check in with yourself when you feel your passion waning. Explore your change of heart. Is it about your business idea or simply the aftermath of a series of tough days?
- Connect with who you are and what you want to do. Your business is an authentic reflection of you and your passion. It must be built on what is truly genuine to you. Don't embark on this journey simply to fulfill others' expectations of you.
- Seek out people who will support you and encourage you to act on your passion.

Vision

BRINGING YOUR IDEA
INTO THE WORLD

What could be worse than being born without sight?
Being born with sight and no vision.

Helen Keller

Vision is the term we use to describe the ability to imagine something that does not yet exist, envision it, and then successfully create it. It is one of the signal traits of successful entrepreneurs—an essential ingredient in getting a business idea off the ground and moving it forward. It is a clear articulation of your passion. Vision is also one of the most powerful motivating forces that enables you to engage and enroll others in bringing forth your dream.

• • • •

Selima Salaun, CEO of Selima Optique in New York's SoHo, has passion; that was clear the moment we met her. She was putting the finishing touches on pieces from her glamorous and witty eyewear collection, which is regularly featured in fashion maga-

21

zines and is collected by trendsetters around the world. But it soon became clear that, fittingly enough, it was Selima's *vision,* fueled by her burning desire that led to her success and acclaim.

"I was an ophthalmologist working in an optical store, a business that I found stale, medical, and serious—not at all fun. And I had a really contrary idea that eyeglasses could be linked with fashion and beauty." Remember "Men don't make passes at women who wear glasses"? That slogan shows how unappealing the notion of eyeglasses used to be. So when Selima started her company in the early 1990s, it was not surprising that people told her she'd never make it because fashion and eyewear just couldn't be mixed.

"It was like saying that if you're a lawyer, you have to wear a black suit. But you can be a great lawyer—and show a little cleavage, too. It seemed obvious to me that the first thing people notice on a person is their glasses. And I knew that there were people who would want glasses with amazing style."

Designer eyewear is so much a part of today's fashion vernacular that you might think it always existed. Not so. Selima led the charge by taking a mundane business that she knew very well and reinterpreting it through the lens of her own creativity and intuition about consumer needs—even before consumers had realized those needs.

When we speak to entrepreneurs like Selima, they talk about having a strong sense of vision, of the "what could be," and having that idea fully formed in their mind's eye. They see a vivid image of a desirable future state that is a marked improvement on that which currently exists, a high-potential business not yet visible to others, almost a prophetic picture of "the possibility." *That's vision.*

"When I opened my first retail store, I couldn't afford to manufacture my own designs. So I bought existing brands and wonderful vintage glasses and mixed the two together, merchandising them in ways never seen before. Everything in my store was important to me—the music, the lighting, the layout—and everything conveyed fashion and fun. It was all part of my vision, how I wanted to bring my concept to life."

Selima's business took off quickly; two years after opening her flagship boutique, she began designing and producing her own branded signature line. Her store was already attracting New York's fashion elite when a top executive from Barney's New York stopped in and bought a pair of "Selima" glasses. Before the end of that day she received a call from them and learned that the store wanted to carry her line. Barney's was the perfect showcase for Selima Optique and the beginning of her expansion to other stores, other coasts, and other countries.

Selima's now employs fifty people in nine stores throughout the United States, Asia, and Europe. She "wanted to make a statement, wanted to show that a woman could make it with a different kind of vision." In her mind's eye, Selima saw the vision of the business she wanted to create; she saw what it would look like and how it would operate. And she was able to distill it into a simple yet profound vision statement: *"To bring fashion and fun to the stale world of retail optical."* And she did.

As Selima says, "With vision and hard work, you can do anything."

. . . .

Your dream may come first, but articulating your passion in the form of a vision is a critical step in building your business because it will have a profound impact on your direction and ultimate success. It will also be a powerful tool in enrolling others in your dream and in your enterprise—future employees, potential customers, and investors, to mention just a few. It will help focus your exploration and research as you determine the feasibility of pursuing your idea.

The first step in bringing your mental picture into the real world is to invest the time and energy to flesh out *your* vision. Without including any numbers, put your thoughts down on paper to help convert your dream into a vision of your business. This vision will serve as an aspirational statement—and a big-picture view of what you wish to achieve.

We've created a simple exercise to help you define and articulate your vision in the Digging Deeper below. (At this time, you may also find it helpful to refer back to your notes from the Chapter 2 Tool Kit exercise, "Can You Turn Your Passion Into a Business?" Part I.)

DIGGING DEEPER

Developing Your Vision

Record your answers to the following questions, but don't worry about how lengthy your initial responses may be. Then go back through your answers and pick out the key elements and compelling words. You may have to repeat this process several times.

1. What does my product, service, or business look like?
2. What do I deliver to my customers?
3. How do I create value for my customers?
4. If I were a customer, what would I want? How can I be sure?
5. What do my competitors offer?
6. What distinguishes my offerings from those of my competitors?
7. What aspects of my business will attract and inspire potential employees?

(continues)

8. Besides getting a paycheck, why would people in my company be excited about their work?
9. When I read my vision statement, what excites me the most about my company?
10. Does my vision stand the test of time? Will what I see today be valid in five years, in ten?

As your company grows and you build its management team, revisit this exercise as a team initiative. Including your team members will ensure that they are aligned with, invested in, and freely participating in your vision for the company.

Important Note: A vision is *not a mission* which describes how, where and for whom you will do your business, e.g. "Selling through distributors to the hospitality industry in North America." It is also *not a strategy* that describes how you will execute your business in a superior manner.

Once you have articulated your vision, the next steps include determining whether your vision can be translated into a sustainable (i.e., profitable) business; and above all, one that will be satisfying to you. Begin by exploring three basic questions—*Is it a real business opportunity? Can I win? Is it worth it?* This process will help you to sort through the myriad possibilities and potential

Can you turn your passion into a business? See Part 2 in the Took Kit, page 179.

opportunities you see before you. You will, in fact, revisit these core questions frequently as your business begins to grow. As you proceed, refer to the Tool Kit: Can You Turn Your Passion into a Business? (Part 2).

IS IT A REAL BUSINESS OPPORTUNITY?

Even Benjamin Franklin's discovery of electricity wasn't a business opportunity until Thomas Edison came up with the light bulb 127 years later. So the first step is to determine *whether* your idea or concept is substantial enough to warrant building an entire enterprise around it. The fundamental question: Is there a big enough market, a unique niche, or an unmet need that will warrant building a full-fledged business? Assuming the market for your product or service is substantial enough to support your idea, ask the following questions: Is my idea *unique* or *different* enough to find acceptance in the marketplace? Can it attract and retain customers? If the product is more commodity-like in nature ask: Can I deliver my product or service "cheaper, better, faster" than the competition and still make a profit? And, finally, if you believe that you can deliver something unique or sufficiently differentiated, the key question becomes: Will my customer *pay* for it?

If your answers to "Is it real?" are a resounding "yes," you are ready to move on to the next question.

CAN I WIN?

Consider these questions: Who competes in the market you are addressing and in your specific niche? What makes your product superior to what's already out there? Do you remember Kate from the beginning of our book—the first time entrepreneur who triumphantly and with complete certainty told us that she had no competition? Believe us, there are few new ideas. And the most potent competition is often what's already in the market or the "tried-and-true" way of doing things. Take Southwest Airlines, for example, which changed the face of airline competition by competing with *ground* transportation rather than other airlines. With its ultra-low fares and lean operations imagine what the bus companies and rental car agencies thought.

If you don't know who can challenge you, or undersell you, you're not only kidding yourself, but you're blatantly telling a potential investor that you don't know your business. Getting a handle on the competitive issues surrounding your business concept is the first major step to playing in the big leagues.

And the issue is broader than simply understanding direct competitors. Professor Michael Porter of the Harvard Business School is a leading expert in the field of competitive analysis and the author of several books on the topic. His model for competitive positioning extends to the threat of new entrants, as well as product substitutes; and the bargaining power of both suppliers and customers.

> *To explore the basic elements that go into an analysis of your competitive position, refer to the Tool Kit to see our outline for a comprehensive competitive analysis*

Determining "can I win" should not be a quick or simple process. If you don't have the answers to these fundamental questions, you'll have a much harder time getting potential clients, investors, or other interested parties to move discussions to the next level.

And now, your most important question:

IS IT WORTH IT?

You've concluded that your business idea is a *real* one and your research informs you that it can be a legitimate *win*. At the end of the day you really want to know whether it will be worth it. Here is another way of looking at it: Will your "Personal Return on Investment"(PROI)—the time, talent, energy, and money (for many, your heart and soul, too)—be enough to warrant the commitment that needs to be made and the risks associated with it? Will it be worth it for you, your investors, your family, and your friends? Ask yourself the soul-searching questions about what are your true goals, your real needs and your *absolute limits*.

This last question is a very personal one. Each individual's risk tolerance and reward ratio is different. Needs, desires, and motivations are unique. For some, they are strictly financial. More often than not, they are broader and involve a bigger universe of considerations. We've seen everything from marriages crumbling to personal bankruptcy. Starting a company may not be worth dismantling your family, taking out a second (or third) mortgage on your home, and risking your life savings and that of your parents and in-laws—all real possibilities. So, take your time and reflect on this one.

That said, most genuinely passionate entrepreneurs can't be stopped no matter how many warning lights flash before them. Some see their vision as "a sign from above" and their mission in life. They're in love. They're obsessed. They're in adrenaline free-fall. Most live by slogans like "Onward and Upward," "Do or Die." We've been there ourselves, and so has every passionate, visionary entrepreneur we know.

If you don't have the answers to these three fundamental questions, get them before going further. If the answer to any one of them is "no," your dream for this business is seriously at risk and you should use these questions to improve your plan, or fold this particular tent and look for another.

If, however, you do conclude your business concept is real, you can win, and it will be worth it to you, it's time to think about how you can effectively communicate your vision to others—to your employees, to prospective customers, to potential investors, to suppliers, and to the various parties who will play a role in its execution. The first and most fundamental vehicle for communicating your vision is a device dubbed the "elevator pitch." You can imagine how it got its name, and hence it is designed to get someone's attention and capture their interest in a very short time.

The elevator pitch is a summary of your vision extended in business terms. It is frequently used in investor, customer, employee, and supplier presentations and tailored to the audience you are addressing. No more than a few sentences long, the "pitch" is a crisp,

> *See Digging Deeper on page 31 for Communicating Your Vision*

compelling synopsis of your company, its business, and its value proposition; it's how to get people interested enough to get on board.

· · · ·

Maria Cirino's vision was just about handed to her on a silver platter by the best of all sources—her customers. Maria had built a remarkably successful career in the high-tech field with her background in sales, marketing, and business development. She learned early on the value of listening to her customers, and it's paid off big time. When she was with two leading-edge technology companies, she watched from a front row seat as all of corporate America moved to embrace that then excitingly new phenomenon—the Internet—that was transforming business and would forever change the face of communications.

As the Web took off, applications grew and usage exploded, outstripping the ability of companies to keep their information secure—and have a safe place to buy and sell, to engage in financial transactions, and to store sensitive data and medical records. Within a span of three years, just about every business application you could think of had shifted to an *unsecure* environment. So, while Maria's Web design and development teams were creating powerful Web sites for their customers, they heard a common refrain: "Can you help us to make it secure?" Well, they couldn't, so those customers were forced to develop their own in-house security systems, a business none of them wanted to be in.

It was clearly a *real* market opportunity. Maria wrapped her vision around this untapped market for Internet security systems and began building her business. With two others, she set about defining the vision around how they would create an "outsourced" Internet security application and how it would be delivered to customers. This product would need constant upgrades, so outsourcing was a natural. Her company would manage and host the application as a remote monitoring system rather than have customers buy, install, and maintain an entire software program that could become obsolete the instant there was a new security threat, or a system was hacked.

The company she envisioned—and created—is called Guardent. It has become the de-facto provider of Internet security systems for financial institutions, telecommunications companies, hospitals, insurance companies, manufacturers, and government agencies, providing necessary products such as firewalls and scanning engines that can stop a security breach before it even occurs. In high-tech-speak, it's what's called a "killer app," or killer application.

As Maria's story illustrates, the biggest piece of your vision should spring from a real need in the market, or solve a real problem. You can't be undisciplined by making your vision too broad; it must be reined in or it will be impossible to execute. So although customers frequently ask Maria to offer other products, she maintains her focus on the core market. She explains the cornerstones of her vision as "the people, the process, and the technology," and although she admits that doing it was harder than she could ever have imagined, today she is in rarified company as one of the few female CEOs of a leading-edge technology enterprise.

By nature, vision is an unknown quantity, and as Maria states, "You can't be afraid of the unknown." On this she is clear: Vision is a constant; it shouldn't change unless your original assumptions are totally off the mark. That doesn't mean that while moving forward there won't be some slight course corrections here and there. But Maria knew she could *win* because she and her team had the technological foundation, the confidence and the contacts, *and* a vision that has remained a constant.

DIGGING DEEPER

Communicating Your Vision

Developing a clear, concise statement that describes the nature of your business in a compelling fashion is the first and most critical step in communicating your vision to others. It must set forth what the company does, for whom, and what benefit it delivers to customers. Condensed to 20 to 30 seconds, it is brief enough to deliver in the time it takes an elevator to reach floor 1—hence, this statement is often referred to as an "elevator pitch." It plays a big role in your networking efforts. Whomever you meet, wherever you meet them, deliver it with energy and enthusiasm and you have a compelling door opener that is sure to get an individual's attention.

Your vision lies at the core of this statement. While brief, it conveys the big picture. It is the hook that piques another party's interest, opening the door to follow up in greater detail. It is a mantra you present when networking with potential customers, employees, investors, vendors, industry peers, advisors and the media. And it has to be consistent across the board.

Vision Statement + Value Proposition = Elevator Pitch

Below is the vision statement for Guardent and examples of elevator pitches corresponding to the various constituents:

"We provide our customers with better information security at lower cost than they could achieve themselves."

(continues)

For customers: "We provide our customers with better information security at a lower cost than they could achieve themselves. If you feel the need to do it better and cheaper, we are your solution."

. . . .

For investors: "We provide our customers with better information security at lower cost than they could achieve themselves. Our market is large and rapidly growing and our product fills a real need. The margins are high, the barriers to entry steep, and we are the trusted provider."

. . . .

For prospective employees: "Our company provides our customers with better information security at a lower cost than they could achieve themselves. We're growing rapidly, we have a great working environment with opportunities for growth and advancement—and we offer outstanding employee benefits."

. . . .

Note: For any such statement, avoid language that might be construed as negative, such as "We can do it better than you." You want to maintain a positive perspective.

Your vision is the starting point as well as the baseline for telling your story. Over time, the communication of your vision will be broadened and will be expressed in multiple forms—mission statements, executive summaries, business plans, annual reports.

. . . .

Unlike Maria, Eva Jeanbart-Lorenzotti had no customers clamoring for the product she envisioned. So how did she create a truly fabulous and successful business? Eva is one of the first people to market luxury products through direct mail catalogs.

Her cosmopolitan upbringing infused her with a passion to bring European style to the United States. She is a perfect example of someone who decided that her business "was worth it." She believed that she "could win," even though only sensing when she started out that her plan "was real." She needed to determine the market feasibility for a brand-new concept and then create the kind of simple yet elegant business idea that makes one say, "Gee, why didn't I think of that?" Early on, it wasn't so easy.

Eva remembers her first "ah-ha moment" back in 1995. She was two years out of business school when she made a startling observation: Catalog sales were enormous in the United States and yet there were no catalogs that sold luxury goods.

Eva knew that Sears, Roebuck and Co. was the first company to successfully use catalogs as a direct marketing vehicle. Perhaps, she thought, because of their humble roots, most catalogs since had a down-market image. She surveyed the landscape and saw a very different possibility, one where luxury goods could be sold through catalogs if they exuded an image of "high quality and style."

The challenge was clear to Eva: "I had to figure out how to convince a group of companies, who on a gut level believed that this medium was wrong for them, that catalogs could not only work for them, they could even enhance their presence. Then I had to figure out how to turn this into a profitable business for everybody involved."

Eva spent six months researching the market. She gathered all the statistics on the catalog business, but focused on the direct-to-consumer segment to determine how big it was, who the major players were, and whether there were competitors in her specific niche. She calculated the investment necessary to get started and asked herself multiple times whether there was really a business behind her idea. In other words, was her plan real? "I wanted to know if there was a luxury catalog on the market, would people find it interesting, would they like it, and most of all, would they buy from it?"

Eva put her initial concept on paper and worked up a mock catalog presentation in storyboard format. She ran focus groups in selected markets—urban centers and well-to-do suburbs—to research her prospective consumers' reactions. "Feedback was clearly positive," Eva recalled, "and I knew then that the idea was doable. What I also knew, however, was that I needed to attract a major upscale brand or two in order to make this whole idea work."

As a result of her research, Eva was able to articulate a compelling vision, that of connecting consumers with the world's top luxury items through the ease of catalog shopping. She tapped into her network, and shared her vision with people who could help her. Through a personal connection, she received an introduction to a major Paris-based manufacturer of high-end silverware. It was none other than Christofle, the perfect candidate for bringing her vision into the marketplace.

She explained to the Christofle executives that she had looked closely at their business and had identified a compelling opportunity. Even though the company had a wonderful line, it had little exposure in the United States. Armed with her extensive market research, she convinced them that direct marketing through catalogs could dramatically extend Christofle's reach in the United States without in any way posing a direct threat to current retail relationships.

It was at the Frankfurt Fair, a major European wholesale show, where Eva traveled down a very long escalator in a very imposing conference center with the man who was then the owner of Christofle's. She recalls, "I told him confidently, 'I'm going to start my catalog business.'" And his response in return, "We'll do it with you."

"I didn't realize what I was saying because I had no employees, no experience, and I had no idea how to start a business. But I had this strong sense of my vision, and now I had one premiere brand backing me. Then I managed to convince another brand to join, and then another and another. Everything that followed was a blur. I just got it done. I made a lot of mistakes, but by October of that year the first catalog was out and 'L'art de Vivre' was a reality."

In the beginning, no one took Eva seriously, not even Eva. She was ahead of the trend in the direct marketing of luxury items, and back then, the direct marketing industry was not as popular or accepted as it is today. "I didn't have a lot of money. I didn't have the press behind me. So it was just me cooking this thing up slowly." We believe it was Eva's clear articulation of the vision for her company and her belief in how it would benefit her customers and partners that was a key factor in her success.

During the next five years, Vivre went from carrying two brands to eight and today it features 140 premier names. There were some life-threatening craters in the road when the economy slumped in 1999 and a partnership with an Internet company almost leveled Vivre. But Eva persevered; today, her original vision still her foundation, her brainchild distributes over 2 million stunning catalogs annually.

Perhaps you're thinking that Eva's business was a groundbreaker and a "really big idea," and that your idea is too small to build into an entire company. Or maybe you're thinking you need to have the next, best, greatest concept—or the solution to world hunger—before you can build a successful enterprise. The truth is that many seemingly small and narrowly focused companies often perform superbly well.

Some of the simplest ideas that make you say "there's never going to be a market for them" or that one silly product can't possibly be a money-making business can actually surprise you. In fact, eBay, a startling success story, began as a Web site built around a passion for collecting PEZ dispensers.

Your idea does, however, have to be big enough to grow into a sustainably profitable enterprise. If your company doesn't make money, it's only a pastime and likely won't last unless you want to keep "feeding it" out of your personal resources (not something we recommend). Every company has its break-even point; that is, when your revenues cover expenses. And when your revenue consistently grows and is significantly greater than your overhead, your business becomes sustainable. You must be able to look at your business model and determine when your venture will hit this important milestone and then know how to secure the wherewithal, financially and otherwise, to get you there.

In addition to profitability and sustainability, there's another critical standard for measuring the success of your enterprise.

YOUR BUSINESS HAS TO REALLY SATISFY YOU

Think about what you'd like your business to look and feel like. What kind of people you want to attract. What values you and your team will live by. Your culture. Consider how your personal and professional needs will be fulfilled and the ways in which you can grow and support your endeavor.

Selima Salaun describes the satisfaction she derives from the business of Selima Optique: "When you strongly believe in your dream and you do everything to make it work—it works. We have nine retail stores and a wholesale business. We sell every-where. I'm still working as much as when I started because I am never satisfied. I always want to do more."

When Maria Cirino of Guardent recounted her stellar list of customers for us, it was clear her business is a success. But what satisfies her the most is the environment she has created for her employees and the feeling of team camaraderie and caring that surrounds everything they do.

Eva Jeanbart-Lorenzotti says of Vivre: "The creation of Vivre has been an unbelievable roller coaster. But, today, we are the only true luxury company in direct marketing, and one of the best high-end catalog marketers. That's my satisfaction."

· · · ·

For others, their entrepreneurial vision is not driven so much by a business opportunity as it is by a sense of purpose or meaning. You may be much like Marcia Weider (whom we profiled in the first chapter) and reach your ultimate vision by asking yourself, "What is really important to me at this time in my life? What has real meaning?"

Jenny Cohen, who had a long and rewarding career in the music industry, became the head of product development at Warner Music International, a division of Warner Brothers. It was then that an inherited kidney disease struck her. Jenny was within a few weeks of dying when a living donor, a total stranger, donated her life-saving organ. "The only way I could deal with this was to think of it as a 'universal gift,' and then I asked myself, 'What am I going to do with it?' Gathering three other like-minded people and forming Songmasters is what Jenny did with what she calls "my second chance."

"Music was always my passion. And, in my eyes, there was an unmet need in the marketplace to find an effective way to connect the substantial marketing dollars of major corporations with worthwhile organizations and causes." Her vision, brought to life by using customized CD-based formats, was to create brand communications and entertainment marketing programs for corporations while significantly benefiting important causes.

"I left the safety net of the corporate life after twenty-four years. Security is nice, but after you've attained it, you realize it's a rather empty destination point. There's a lot of work to be done on a service or a spiritual level and I think it's a critical time to be thinking of creative ways to take current structures and systems and to use them to do something important.

"I have moments of fear and panic where I think, 'How did I get myself out on this limb? And is there any way but going further out on it?' Of course, we took a major leap of faith starting Songmasters. If it were a sure thing, it wouldn't be entrepreneurial. Leaping is the nature of vision. You have to be heading to a horizon that only you can see. And your job is to hold onto that vision and be flexible, allowing for changes to happen because you're being taught by your experience."

And this brings us to our last point.

As part of your vision, be clear, very clear, about why you're starting a business.

Some people start a business because they want to make money; for others, it is a way of proving something to themselves or others. Some want independence and autonomy; others the sheer thrill of competition. Many want to change the world, to be the absolute best in their fields, or simply to experience the sweet satisfaction of creating something that has never been done before.

Now, with a strong sense of your vision in place, you can refer to the Tool Kit, which gives more information and provides outlines of the key pieces that are used in communicating your vision to the outside world. The Tool Kit contains an outline for the Executive Summary, the standard tool for explaining your business to potential investors and others. It's a great place to begin putting the necessary ingredients of your vision into the framework of the key elements: your market, your product, and your competitive environment. We have included an actual Executive Summary for reference, and an outline for an Investor Power Point presentation (which will be discussed in Chapter 6).

Further, as you build upon your vision and recruit others to help make it a reality, there are instances, especially in the technology world, where you will want and need to protect your proprietary information. Please refer to the section on Non Disclosure Agreements, or NDAs in the Tool Kit, if they are appropriate to your situation. Don't be reticent in talking about your idea and networking to make it happen. A vision will never evolve into a reality if nobody knows about it.

. . . .

We've explored a lot of stories and examples around vision because we think it's that important. In *Built to Last,* a business classic first published in 1995, two Stanford professors, James Collins and Jerry Porras, report that the stock market returns of "visionary" companies (those created and guided by strong and clear visions) outperformed those without by nearly seven times. Combined with execution, vision clearly will enable you to progress and succeed as you go forward.

And don't forget to think about what's motivating you to go out on your own. *Is it a real business? Can you win? Is it worth it? Will it satisfy you?* In the next chapter, we'll look at what it means to be a pioneer in the business sense of the word. We'll explore the hallmarks of successful "pioneers" as we introduce you to two entrepreneurs whose visions led them to experience first-hand the thrills, frustrations, and rewards of breaking new ground.

WHAT YOU NEED TO KNOW

- Tap into your "mind's eye" to envision your product or company. Begin to define and articulate it in concrete terms.
- Drawing upon your vision, develop a Vision Statement around what your company will deliver and how. Your vision serves as the ultimate point you are aiming for on the horizon.
- Distill your vision into a short, inspirational statement, for example, "Ladies and Gentlemen Serving Ladies and Gentlemen" (Ritz Carlton Hotels); or "To Create a Place Where We Can All Be Kids" (Disney Theme Parks). Road-test your vision statement with others. Is it clear? Does it inspire?
- From your vision statement, craft an elevator pitch that creates immediate interest among desired constituents and compels them to ask for more information on the company. Although your vision should remain fixed, your elevator pitch will evolve as the business grows. Revise and refine it accordingly, particularly in the early days.

- Organize your vision into executable "milestones" (i.e., specific steps to be accomplished in an orderly fashion) and manage your business and your time to achieve them. We'll talk more about this critical execution step in the next chapter.
- Don't hide your vision under a rock. Discussing your vision openly is the key to turning it into a business.
- Don't be discouraged by look-alikes or by new entrants into your market. Success ultimately depends on your ability to execute your plan. However, do revisit your assumptions about the market opportunity when you hear about or see new competitors. The downside of their presence is that they could eat your lunch. The upside: Your vision has been validated by your competitors, whose efforts may actually expand demand for your product or service.
- Watch for wishful thinking; don't allow it to cause you to turn a blind eye to marketplace data that doesn't support your idea. Keep your mind open as you see data or hear feedback about your business vision.
- Make sure your vision is focused and disciplined. If you are all over the place with your vision, you'll never get anywhere.
- At this stage, it is worthwhile to step back and take the time to reflect on what is motivating you.
- When considering your "PROI"—your Personal Return on Investment—discuss your vision with family, friends, and respected colleagues. Gain their perspective and input, and freely ask for their support.

Pioneering Spirit

DISCOVERING NEW FRONTIERS

Aerodynamically, the bumble bee shouldn't be able to fly, but the bumble bee doesn't know that, so it goes on flying anyway.

Mary Kay Ash

The drive to innovate, build, or conquer that results in the development of a new technology or the twisting of an old paradigm, so that the business of daily life is forever changed, is the fuel for some entrepreneurs. For others, the breakthrough to a new commercial venture could be as simple and dramatic as noticing a particular busy intersection and envisioning a gourmet coffee shop on the northwest corner. Built on both passion and vision, we call this drive to break new ground *pioneering spirit*, a necessary third ingredient as you create and give rise to your enterprise. We don't want to imply that being a pioneer entails being a loner and an isolationist. Rather, you are one star in a much larger constellation. Those who possess the pioneering spirit experience an invigorating life journey that offers risk and opportunity and always results in personal growth and strong emotions.

. . . .

It was 6:00 A.M., and Sharon Whiteley, a serial entrepreneur and coauthor of this book, was in the flight lounge at Logan International Airport on her way to the San Francisco office of Third Age. Third Age is an interactive online community that serves the needs and interests of aging baby boomers and companies that are interested in marketing to this growing audience. 8Wings Ventures LLC had recently invested in this early-stage company and Sharon, enthusiastic about the opportunity, agreed to take on the job of CEO.

A fellow business traveler recalled being in another airport with Sharon. "We'd been in Israel for two weeks and were getting ready to come back to the States. All I wanted to do was get a Coke and a slice of pizza, sit down, and wait for the plane. But there was a small retail arcade way down at the other end of the terminal and Sharon could not sit still until she'd traversed it. Twenty minutes later, she was back with a ton of new ideas for businesses. That's what the pioneering spirit looks like. Sharon has a sixth sense around sizing up a market and figuring out what to sell into it. She's like a human, commercial homing device."

Sharon laughed at this description, but admitted that it's true. Entrepreneurs like her feel vibrantly alive when they're discovering a new market, creating a new product or service, or when they're revitalizing an old business idea by illuminating it with a different-colored light. They have a hunger to push the limits of what's been done before and, as the old landscape disappears in the rear view mirror, they get a rush from mastering new survival skills as they press on toward the unknown.

Back at Logan Airport, Sharon powered off her cell phone and laptop and then recalled the beginning of the business, Peacock Papers, she had conceived, launched, funded, and led for fourteen years:

By most standards, I was already a very successful entrepreneur. I had founded and built two profitable companies and was flourishing in an exciting career in the specialty shopping center development industry. I was earning a lot of money and was receiving accolades for my accomplishments. But, at the same time, my passion was starting to wane. I was getting bored and, as I look back, unconsciously I had already started looking for another mountain to climb. Even new and challenging opportunities in my field left me feeling "been there, done that."

It was during this time that I started what I call a "quirky habit of collecting sayings." Some were headlines from advertisements, others were phrases or aphorisms that struck me as particularly insightful or inspirational. I found myself making makeshift cards, even framing some, and sending them on to friends and family.

Then one day I came across a headline that read, *"A Peacock That Sits on Its Tail Feathers Is Just Another Turkey."* It was a showstopper for me. For starters, my maiden name, Pfau, means "peacock" in a few languages, so anything with the word or graphic of a peacock always got my attention. As silly as it may sound, I read this message as a sign.

So that weekend, I sequestered myself in my office at home and drafted a skeleton business plan for what six months later became Peacock Papers, a greeting card and party invitation company. I invested everything I had. I borrowed as much as I could, signed away my life for even more—and then I incorporated.

From the beginning, Peacock's unique appeal distinguished it from the highly competitive world of Hallmark, American Greetings, and newer alternative greeting card companies such as Recycled Paper. Peacock's product line consisted of typographically designed message cards and companion party invitations in an easy-to-send four-by-six flatcard format. More traditionally viewed as postcards, these distinctively rendered phrases were marketed unusually as well, the Peacock-embossed envelopes ensuring a sender's privacy.

The research Sharon did in advance of setting out on this venture was "hardly scientific," as she puts it. Rather, she attributes her ability to size up the market, assess the competition, and ferret out opportunities to her preexisting and deep knowledge of retailing and what she learned from the reactions of those who received her early cards. Her gut told her that because people's lives were becoming busier and time more precious, they wanted an easy but still meaningful way to communicate with others. The "quick send" vehicle she'd designed was straightforward and easy for senders to use.

You may be wondering why Sharon did not perform traditional "market research" to the same extent that other entrepreneurs do (such as Eva, discussed in the last chapter). We find that the amount and kind of research and preparation that entrepreneurs do before starting out can range from highly intuitive (like Sharon's) to extensive research involving interviews with potential customers, the analysis of similar companies, and so on. It is a matter of one's style, personality, and experience. Sharon's ability to "jump in" stems from trusting her gut instincts and her experience as an entrepreneur.

Sharon's intuition paid off, and out of this successful first-product release came a series of other firsts in her product line.

Peacock was the first to silk screen and box high-quality T-shirts as gifts; the first to create positive messaging on an array of products celebrating aging; and, probably in one of its most innovative firsts, Peacock created metallic confetti, branded as "Confettios."

Entrepreneurs possess a sense of market readiness, an internal radar system that is always scanning the environment for new information.

Whether the idea is brand-new or a new spin on an old top, entrepreneurs are market-driven; that is, they are drawn in and sensitive to the supply-and-demand flow of the marketplace. They develop an all-consuming relationship with the world and a corollary view to its impact on a potential business. Some see a billboard and imagine their ads going there. Some meet a new person and wonder whether he or she could be a potential customer, backer, or supplier. They are excited by the potential of each new dawn: "With a new business, every day is an adventure. I felt like I was flying on a trapeze without a safety net below," says Sharon.

"Eventually, the business of running Peacock became routine for me. When we came to the end of our spiraling growth stage, we bought and subsequently merged with a large, established paper tableware manufacturer with whom we had developed an earlier successful licensing relationship. It was lucky for me, very lucky, because exit strategies were nowhere on my radar screen when I first fell in love with the possibility for creating Peacock."

Like all explorers, Sharon was willing to take action without guarantees. Those with a pioneering spirit don't often think in terms of exit strategies because they believe in themselves and in their business idea, more than in the risk factors involved.

Cynthia Fisher, former CEO and founder of Viacord and Via-Cell, is a trailblazer of the highest order. With the help of her B.A. in biophysics and M.B.A. from Harvard, she became a pioneer in a new industry. When Cynthia's revolutionary work began in 1993, it was practically unknown that blood from the umbilical cord is rich in precious stem cells that can be used to repair cellular damage, restore marrow function after chemotherapy, and fight diseases such as leukemia, sickle cell anemia, lymphoma, and certain genetic disorders. Viacord is oriented to the consumer by making it possible for families to bank cord blood for future use by the newborn or their families; ViaCell provides stem cells from the umbilical cord to the medical community.

Cynthia's journey to the forefront of medical science began at home. "My grandparents, a close cousin, and my sister in particular all experienced extremely debilitating and life-threatening diseases. My dream for Viacord and ViaCell was to make a real difference to people's health and lives from a survival standpoint. I saw that it was possible in many cases to deliver an affordable and curative therapy to help people live."

In the early 1990s, when she was marketing director at Haemonetics—a company that makes equipment used in the collection of blood products—Cynthia had a brilliant flash of insight. She knew that umbilical cord blood, which is discarded after a child's birth, was tremendously rich in stem cells, a valuable resource that could be stored for future use in cancer patients. But there was no link between oncologists and obstetricians. Cynthia saw this gap and envisioned a new kind of company that would bridge it.

"Harvesting bone marrow for stem cells entailed very painful surgery for the donors, was extremely expensive for the patients, and effective only about 40 percent of the time. I just kept thinking, if you could just get the cord blood that's thrown out with the placenta in every delivery, we wouldn't need these horrific marrow transplant procedures and you get the stem cells with a 100 percent transplantation rate at a much lower cost."

The price of Cynthia's cord-blood banking service would be a one-time $1,500 collection charge and an annual storage fee of $95, affordable compared to the $25,000 needed to harvest bone marrow, a procedure most insurance plans don't cover.

"I thought if everybody had the choice to save their own child's cord blood, it would be biological insurance for the child and the family if it was ever needed. And wouldn't that be great? This was the dream that enabled me to fight the hard fight—the dream that would demand pioneering new fields with a tremendous number of unforeseen obstacles that were not obvious starting out."

In technology, a company's future begins with securing a competitive advantage through patents. Cynthia learned that a patent on cord-blood collection that was very broad in scope already existed. "I thought the patent hurdle was a big one to overcome, but when I look back now, it was nothing in comparison to the other obstacles that lay ahead."

Through years of discouraging setbacks, during which time Cynthia put in more than a million dollars of her own and family money, she was able to disengage her piece of the new technology from that old patent and secure her own. Then she and her partners went to the Food and Drug Administration (FDA) *sixteen times* before launching their commercial cord-blood stem cell banking service, still without that agency's help or approval.

"We were given no cooperation from the FDA, let alone any guidance on regulating this new field, which would have been helpful, so we just took off without it. News spread and we received major network coverage—the press thought we were pretty spectacular. It was right after we received this prime-time media exposure that the FDA proposed new regulations for harvesting stem cells; they would allow the non-profit competitors who clearly wanted to enter our field to do so and thus present a difficult competitive challenge that would have stopped us in our tracks."

Cynthia took the money that had been tagged for marketing campaigns to grow the business and put it toward regulatory counsel, legislative counsel, and the FDA reform bill. "In the meantime, I ran a Ralph Nader–like grassroots campaign. I wrote to physicians and got the lobbying power of the major cancer centers to understand how this proposed regulation would be detrimental to their bone marrow transplant programs. It was not just our company that was at risk. The legislation would actually impose really strict regulations on the medical profession at large."

During this battle for the company's life, hundreds of letters and substantiating documents were sent to challenge the proposed legislation. They came from all over—from Viacord's patient families, from obstetricians, from researchers at bone marrow transplant centers, and from transplant physicians at hospitals such as Children's Hospital and Mass General in Boston—impressive hospitals that supported the proposed Viacord model.

"Thanks to this grassroots effort, we beat the FDA challenges, but it didn't end there. After we won the FDA battles, we ran into opposition from the Red Cross and other non-profit competitors who thought they could use the grinding machinery and bureaucracy of the Federal Trade Commission (FTC) to ultimately frustrate us so much that we'd shut our doors. It was ludicrous. Two years and another $250,000 later, we finally prevailed in this battle and were home free. We won."

And she won big.

In mid-2000, Cynthia merged her business with a like-minded partner, and the new company raised $80 million in investment capital. They doubled their staff and Cynthia saw the early success of her company when five customers' lives were saved by cord blood.

Some entrepreneurs who, like Cynthia Fisher, have scientific minds prefer to play in a technical field. Some have a genius for financial products; others, for new inventions. But 90 percent of successful ventures are old ideas, refurbished or reinvented with a fresh new coat of better-faster-cheaper paint.

Still, risk is inseparable from the act of starting a new venture.

As Jenny Cohen reminded us, "If there were guarantees, it wouldn't be entrepreneurial." You may not think of yourself as a pioneering spirit—or a risk taker—so let's look at the risk factors from all sides, balancing the rewards and excitement of starting a potentially successful business with some of the downsides that an enthusiastic pioneering spirit may choose to ignore.

First, the most obvious risk is financial. Initially, you've got to fund your venture yourself, because if you don't put "your own skin in the game" it will be nearly impossible to persuade others to invest in your venture. You're at financial risk if you're quitting a job that provides a steady paycheck, or hocking your house, or draining your bank account. Your decision also affects the people around you who may depend on you for financial support, or at least for financial accompaniment.

There's more. Your ego is at risk: If your better mousetrap doesn't work or your catering business tanks, your self-esteem suffers the blow. For now, you *are* your business vision; in the eyes of the world, depending on the outcome, you're either a hero or a bum. It's tough for some people to deflect this kind of critical judgment and retain an optimistic attitude.

You also risk your professional reputation. A business failure could hurt your standing in the business community, making it that much harder to attract future opportunities. Your bankable credentials in your "paying job" may not translate readily to your new venture. If you've left a job or industry and later decide to go back, some bright and younger superstar may have taken your place in line.

Last, there's what we call "lifestyle risk." This isn't about money. It's about how you've changed. The very act of going out on your own changes your relationships with everyone around you.

Just as you've told all your friends and neighbors and business colleagues and the food industry press that you're going into the catering business, your power base has shrunk to the size of a cell phone. You're running a business out of a shoebox of an office or your spare bedroom. You fly coach these days, and the people who used to return your calls when you were a senior VP at Humongous, Inc., don't return your phone calls anymore.

Or let's say you're a huge success. You're the next Forbes Magazine Entrepreneur of the Year, working a hundred hours a week, a cell phone glued to your ear. You're flying from somewhere to somewhere else and are never home. Perhaps your partner (or children or friends) didn't sign on for the sacrifices that go with picking up the home court slack for the entrepreneur of the year.

Entrepreneurs don't go into a business thinking that they'll fail. Put your money on the line in Vegas and the odds are stacked against you, even if you've played roulette before, even if you're very lucky. When you start a business, the machines aren't rigged. You are a primary factor in whether you succeed or fail, and the way you operate your business affects your chances. You've got to use all five of your senses and the market-reading radar that entrepreneurs with a strong sense of pioneering spirit use as a sixth sense.

Think about this, too: The risks of a pioneering adventure in the world of entrepreneurship could be fewer than those the status quo represents. It may be risky to start a business, but staying in your humdrum but well-paying job may be just as risky. You may not get that promotion. You may not be the one who succeeds the president. Your company may find itself in the midst of a business scandal and you lose your job. Corporate downsizing is legion today and no one has the guaranteed lifetime employment that could be expected twenty years ago.

Change happens. You face risk with any major life transition, and most people will face all the risks we mentioned for entrepreneurs at some time in their lives. But here's what you stand to gain when you become an entrepreneur: You'll have a real sense of independence. Although there may be partners and investors weighing in from the sidelines, you will be running the show. You'll have more control over your agenda, your work environment, and your destiny. You will be the ultimate decisionmaker in how you execute your business. You will be the guardian of your vision.

Regardless of the outcome, you will be taking on personal growth. Even if your business falls short of your dreams, you will have acquired new skills and perspectives that you can use to start another business some day. Your experience makes you even more valuable to the marketplace, and although you might lose your place in the job line, you *will* earn money again. And maybe you'll find a more rewarding way in which to do it.

Finally, we don't think the issue is, "Should I throw away my career to start a new business?" We think of starting a business as advancing your career in a different direction. Many people looking at entrepreneurs view their walk on the wild side as risky, but entrepreneurs don't think of their business ventures this way. Their pioneering spirit leads them to a different way of assessing risk.

Bored by the status quo, entrepreneurs accept risk as the field on which the game is played. For an entrepreneur, risk is akin to diving off a cliff with a bungee cord tied to an ankle. Sure, the cord could break, but it won't break for me.

Cynthia Fisher recalled the hardships she faced when she started her business:

> There's so much personal growth and so much personal sacrifice involved that the payoff is the journey. There were times when staying afloat was so, so hard. I didn't take a salary for seven years and didn't know if we could keep going until the next day. Somehow, the next day came and I'd say, "Okay, I'll reach into my pocket. We'll meet the payroll. We'll figure out how to get to next week." I loved my company and the work we were doing, but if things had gone irretrievably against us and I'd had to walk away and eat humble pie, I'd happily have eaten humble pie. Succeed or fail, the experience is just as rich in personal growth.

Know that entrepreneurs aren't daredevils. They are optimists. They see the upside potential and calculate the risk in each of the categories we have outlined. They believe that their businesses will ultimately be financially rewarding as well as emotionally gratifying, the optimal vehicle for achieving their deepest goals, for making their dreams come true. And often those dreams do come true.

Entrepreneurs are in the race to win; as they push themselves to go the distance, they want feedback on their progress as they go.

Ed Koch, the former mayor of New York City, used to ask at every press conference, "How am I doing?" Entrepreneurs are like that. They want to know how they're doing personally and how their product is being received. They set milestones for themselves so that they can sharpen their tools and improve their performance. Entrepreneurs thrive on concrete action and progress. They need to make it happen—to execute, plain and simple. Feedback gives them critical data so that they can correct course if necessary. And *favorable* feedback supplies the nourishment they need to keep pushing forward.

DIGGING DEEPER

Milestone Overview

According to the *American Heritage Dictionary,* a milestone is a "stone marker set up on a roadway to indicate the distance in miles from a given point." For the start-up company, milestones represent discrete, measurable, and time-specific achievements that serve as the building blocks of the business. The entrepreneur will use milestones to: (1) translate the business plan into tactical steps that can be executed; (2) grow the business to reach profitability; and (3) increase the economic value of the business at each stage of development. Additionally, milestones function as markers, concrete and visible "wins" that keep the entrepreneur focused, disciplined, and on course vis-à-vis the broader business vision. Inwardly, milestones provide a sense of sustenance and help build momentum. When you reach a mile-

(continues)

stone, your sense of what can be achieved through the business is expanded, providing fuel for your continued march.

When setting milestones, avoid the trap of feeling that they must be
achievements on a grand scale. Rather, effective milestone setting simply requires identifying progress benchmarks that can be defined,
quantified, and accomplished as an integral part of moving the business forward and increasing its value. Bear in mind that when the time
comes to raise capital, investors will link funding to the achievement
of specific milestones that will increase the valuation of the company.

Although the nature, and underlying details, of milestones will be
specific to your particular business, milestones are generally orga-
nized into categories that mirror the functional areas of the business:
Strategic, Financial, Product Development, Sales and Marketing,
Operations, Human Resources, and so on. A sample of a milestone-
setting exercise in the Product Development area can be found in
the Tool Kit on page 193.

There are different milestones for different businesses. But in
general, innovative thinking, measurable progress, taking calculated risks, having a solid management team, and showing financial responsibility are of keen interest to potential investors,
many of whom won't back someone who hasn't started a company, built a company, and sold a company successfully. Not
that past performance guarantees future performance or a positive outcome; concrete data points and forward progress are still
important. Soon the internal need to measure how you're doing
will become an external necessity as well.

. . . .

In the next chapter we will look at tenacity, that steadfast determination that somehow springs eternal when your tank is all

but empty—that desire and energy to persevere, even in the daunting face of adversity. It's innate in entrepreneurs and it's a good thing because sometimes it's all you've got.

WHAT YOU NEED TO KNOW

- Uncertainty about where to start can paralyze first-time entrepreneurs from taking action. Have your initial goals and the early milestones you want to reach in place to help you to prioritize your actions.
- Market research comes in many forms and is found in many places. Don't underestimate the value of past experiences because they contribute to your perspectives.
- Make order out of chaos. In the early months, each day passes in a blur of activity that may seem unrelated to your original idea or your goals. This is normal.
- Regularly examine how you are spending your time and re-order your priorities as needed. You are constantly bombarded with opportunities for distraction. Even when it seems there is no time to stop and reflect, take a break, even for a minute or two, to regain your focus. You will see an exponential return on these reflective moments.
- The customer always comes first. Make a practice of returning customers' calls and dealing with their issues promptly.
- Establish a strong network of support, whether it's an advisory board or a kitchen cabinet. With your singular focus on building your company, isolation can sometimes be a by-product of the entrepreneurial life.
- Among your advisors, include someone who sold to your target market or has experience in functional areas that are important to your business.

- Poor judgment, bad decisions, and just plain old mistakes are part of the every day entrepreneurial experience. These are forms of feedback; recognize them as such and learn from them.
- In hindsight, you will be tempted to second-guess yourself. Try to remember that at the time you made a particular decision, you made it with the information you had available to you. It is better to make a decision than stay frozen in the tracks of uncertainty.
- You never feel as good about your successes to the same extent as you feel bad about your failures. Remember to cut yourself some slack.
- Trust your intuition.

Tenacity

PASSION'S BULLDOG

Life is not easy for any of us. But what of that? We must have perseverance and above all confidence in ourselves.

Marie Curie

In the beginning, there comes a moment when you notice that you're onstage alone. You're holding the mike and singing your heart out, but apart from the rowdies in the front row, you're playing to an empty house. Realization dawns. No one really cares about your business idea but you. Some time in the future, the marketplace may flock to your good idea, but despite conventional wisdom, building a better mousetrap doesn't guarantee that the world will beat a path to your door. *There are no guarantees,* but this we know: Your success depends on your commitment to your idea.

. . . .

It's funny how when you just start out, you have triumphs one day, despair the next. Later, when you *really* get going, you'll have triumph and despair on the *same day, every day.* And throughout the entire roller-coaster ride, you must keep your head up and your eye on that fixed point you've glued to the horizon if you are to find the positive energy you need to keep moving ever forward.

To win, you must have tenacity.

You must persevere.

Tenacity is more than dogged determination, although it's that too. Tenacity embodies an optimism that is endemic to entrepreneurs. It's how you find the confidence to drum up the seed money and get up on that stage to begin with. And there's a kind of fierceness in tenacity, a resolve to win, despite the risk of present or future failure.

As one entrepreneur said recently, "There were days when I was too depressed to even get out of bed, but I got up anyway because I knew if I didn't carry the flag, my company would die."

Right. That's true.

And that's why, first and foremost, understanding the compelling nature of your vision is essential to your success. It's up to you to convince the world that your product or service is the solution to a problem—the more painful the better—or the pathway to an expanded existence, that you have a concept that fills an unmet need or addresses one that has already been filled, but yours does it in a more innovative, efficient, faster, or cost-effective way.

You must also convince *yourself*, because your commitment to this vision will be tested when, inevitably, things take longer than they should and cost more than you thought they would; or when a global event shakes out the economy like an old dust rag; or when the notorious quirkiness of human nature causes someone to gum up the works.

Occasionally, that quirky someone is you.

This is how it was for Robin Chase. Robin had an idea for a new kind of rental car business. She called it Zipcar. The way she imagined it, cars would be parked throughout a city, available to club members by the hour. Environmentally friendly, Zipcars would make it possible for city dwellers to get around without the cost, upkeep, or responsibility of owning a car; and the city would benefit from fewer cars on the roads and less pollution from the ones that were.

Robin refined her business model, hired a staff, purchased her fleet of sparkling green VW bugs, and signed up Zipcar club members. The city of Boston liked her idea so much that it donated parking spots in municipal lots. Along the way, Robin faced her share of heckling rowdies, but in time she convinced investors that Zipcars were the wheels of the future. Angel investors pledged $1.3 million to fund the expansion of Robin's dream. Three weeks before the much-needed funding was to arrive, just when everything was going smoothly, Robin noticed that something was terribly wrong:

> I was building the company during the dot-com demise. Bodies of failed entrepreneurs littered the landscape and I was constantly measuring myself against that; cautioning myself not to be that careless or that foolish or that optimistic or that blind that I too could fall into a trap. So I was very focused on the business model, always asking myself, "*Is this something that can really work?*"
>
> I was running the business out of my home; six of us were jammed into the spare bedroom and I remember clearly the moment when the floor fell through. I was looking at our monthly revenues and at what our receivables should be for that level of activity—and the revenue just wasn't there.

It was an abominable moment; absolute rock bottom for me when I saw that what I'd been espousing and reality were actually very far from aligned. And I thought, "This isn't going to work. I fooled all the investors and spent all this time and got cars and got members and this deal is just not viable."

I didn't say anything at first. I even kept it together when one of my investors called. But then I put down the phone, went to my bedroom and closed the door, pulled the curtains across the windows, threw myself on the bed, and just cried for the rest of the day. I didn't know yet where the mistake had happened or what, in fact, it was; but I just kept thinking, "What have I done? And how am I going to get out of this?" I knew that I would have to do it. It was like being in labor. Or like going down a narrow one-way street. Like it or not, there was no turning back.

Robin spent the rest of the day weeping, but eventually she pulled herself together, washed her face, combed her hair, and went back to work. She's pretty tough on herself, especially when it comes to what she calls "intellectual honesty." That means looking at the numbers and paying attention to what she found. Robin knew this wasn't the time for denial:

People frequently say of entrepreneurs, "Don't believe your own tales." And I completely agree. I threw myself into intense financial analysis mode and hunted down the holes in my earlier thinking. It seems so obvious now. We had projected revenues based on hourly rentals and somehow all of us, even our investors, had overlooked the effect of our discounted daily rentals. This meant that our revenues would be at least 30 percent lower than we had projected. We wouldn't be able to fulfill our hiring plans, let alone project a profit. It was a disaster.

I spent the next three or four days realigning reality and scrupulously determining what I could produce, and I also spent a lot of time convincing myself once more that Zipcar was viable. I reworked the numbers, adjusted our pricing, changed dramatically how I projected future revenue—and finally arrived at the point where I could say, "Okay, I can do this."

The road would be much longer than Robin once planned. That's where the tenacity and the painful perseverance comes in. "I had to go through the pain. It was demoralizing personally and embarrassing, but my good name and my reputation had been flung out there, and I had investors and members and staff who were counting on me. I had to make it right."

And she did. There are now over a hundred Zipcars in the Boston fleet alone, their drivers honking hello to one another as they pass on the roadway. New fleets have been started in Washington, D.C., and New York, and expansion into Denver and San Francisco is on the agenda. There are over 5,550 Zipcar "members" as we write this. Zipcars are green, and they're also in the black—thanks to Robin's tenacity.

We know that tenacity begins in conviction and is fueled by passion. When it's manifested as positive perseverance, it absorbs the interference, as it did for Robin, so that you can tackle new information, pluck the learning element from it, reposition, and re-strategize. *Tenacity helps you see around obstacles or cut through them so that you can win.*

Some would say that entrepreneurs don't consider themselves tenacious. They are as oblivious to their tenacity as fish are to water. It's the environment they live in. It's just the way they *are*.

Tenacity, thy name is Judy George.

From the time she was a young girl, Judy was in love with interior design. While school friends were taping pictures of the Beatles to their walls, Judy was covering hers with pictures of well-furnished rooms. When she was a thirty-four-year-old mother of four, Judy's passion was inflamed by a new and forward-thinking company in town, Hamilton Home Décor, and she was determined to work for them. When her resume and letters failed to win her an interview with CEO George Hamilton, Judy used methods the likes of which have rarely been seen before or since.

Judy "borrowed" $10,000 from her husband's bank account. Then she hired a plane that trailed an advertising banner reading "Hire Judy George—She'll Make You Millions" to fly by Hamilton's offices daily. When Hamilton's cease-and-desist order didn't make Judy go away, he gave her a job—and she rewarded his decision by rising quickly from director of the company's design studio to senior vice president in one year. After Hamilton passed away, the company was sold to Scandinavian Design, and within five years, Judy became president. She then pitched an idea that had been living fully formed in her mind for years. It was for a new division and a brand new way to merchandise furniture: "My new boss and I were kind of driving each other crazy. He was making a fortune and the company was successful, but I had an idea for packaging romantic *collections* of home furnishings and I wanted to start a division around this concept. I wanted the company to give me the seed money so that I could run with it. I'd long thought that if I stayed on board and helped him live his dream, he'd help me live mine."

That's why Judy was very excited when she was called to a meeting on a bright Saturday morning in the summer of 1986. Thinking that she was about to be given the green light on her subsidiary business, Judy invited fifty friends to dinner that night to celebrate her imminent elevation.

Instead, she was fired.

Judy can laugh about this now: "I hadn't realized what a thorn I'd been in my boss's side." And we have the feeling she took this blow in stride even then. To begin with, Judy put on her slinky black dress and threw the dinner party anyway. Then, while folding one tent, Judy pitched another. She turned her energy to raising money for a business of her own. "I had to raise millions, and having not been a CEO, but just a president, and in an industry where venture capitalists said, 'Never give a woman money,' it wouldn't be as easy as wishing on a star."

It was clear to Judy that she would need help in figuring out how to launch her business, and asking for that help took courage. "I got advice. I hired a film crew and the best advertising agency I could find. Then we went all over the United States and filmed customers who were going to be *my* customers."

Judy interviewed women coming out of department stores, furniture stores, and boutiques all over the country. She asked them how they felt about their homes and was moved by their stories. When she asked them what it was like to buy furniture, women told her that what should have been exciting and pleasurable was pretty near defeating. Furniture stores were typically stocked with rows and rows of unrelated furniture and manned by slick salesmen; and then the customer had to wait at home all day for her delivery. Judy knew that this wasn't how buyers wanted to be sold and treated.

"I took all that information and made a spectacular ten-minute video. I put it together with a business plan and got the $3.5 million I needed in fewer than six months. I was fired in July and I had my first two stores open the following year."

Fifteen years later, Domain is recognized as a national leader in the highly competitive home furnishings arena. With twenty-five stores in the chain, it's surpassing $70 million in annual revenues. In 2002, the company was sold to a leading international retail giant. Judy now sits on its board of directors, the first female director in the company's history.

"You know, along the way, I made every mistake I could possibly make," Judy continued. "I spent all the money, then got more. I persevered and I kept coming up to bat, and my backers knew I was going to hit a home run for them with it. I raised a total of 28 million dollars and I believe I was largely able to do this because of my tenacious personality. That, and of course, people loved my concept."

But what if people don't find your tenacity endearing? Don't love your business concept? What if your detractors say, "It's too expensive, too cheap, too late." Or, as some said to Robin Chase, "I had the same idea five years ago. And, by the way, Americans love their cars. There's not a snowball's chance in hell your idea will work."

We'll admit that tenacity involves a bit of positive denial, a way of looking at the recent setback as a temporary detour, not the end of the road. But no good comes from ignoring red flags. Sometimes the bridge really *is* out.

When critics told Robin Chase about their "same idea five years ago," she could laugh: *Having* the idea and *doing* the idea are two different things. But, "Americans love their cars and Zipcar doesn't have a snowball's chance in hell" was a different kind of criticism. Robin had to check that by asking questions: Is this criticism true? Why did I start the Zipcar business in the first place? What was the benefit or unique value proposition that made me think that Americans would embrace an alternative to car ownership?

If you are committed to your idea and believe in yourself, you can hear criticism, ask questions, and even process negative information. That's how you'll find a new way to skin the cat. We've all heard about the swashbuckling sort of entrepreneur who gets an idea and forges ahead, no matter what, and we take issue with that stereotype.

We applaud positive perseverance, yes. We encourage tenacity in the face of setbacks, absolutely. Never say die, never give up the ship, damn the torpedoes, full speed ahead—all are great battle cries. But we don't endorse beating your head repeatedly against the same wall until you knock yourself senseless. Blind stubbornness or obstinacy extinguishes innumerable infant businesses.

Take, for instance, a young entrepreneur who came to us for funding in 2001. We'll call her Karen Finn. She was smart, highly motivated, and had a pretty interesting business: online classifieds. But Karen couldn't accept what potential investors kept telling her: The valuation she assigned to her business was too high for such an early stage of development, too high for her management team's lack of work experience, and too high because she had no proven track record of building a business.

Despite very specific and repetitive feedback from us and others in the investment community to this effect, Karen dug in and became obstinate about her position. She never stopped to reexamine the valuation or to revisit her expectations. She didn't even compare her company's valuation to that of companies of similar size and stage of development or of others in the same industry. The result: Because she alienated potential investors, Karen got no funding. And worse, because she had tar-

For a more detailed explanation on valuation and why it is so important when you raise outside investment capital, see "Digging Deeper" on valuation, page 74

nished her reputation and weakened her credibility with the investment community, it would be very difficult to come back in the future with a new plan or a new business idea.

If only Karen had been able to take in the feedback long enough to ask herself whether the criticism was true or untrue, to test her original assumptions, and to step back from her original business model and consider other ways to make it work.

We would like to have seen her ask the following types of questions: Why is the feedback from these investors consistently at odds with my view? Are there proven strategic partners I can affiliate with to strengthen my chances for success and enhance my valuation? Are there complementary products I can offer through the same distribution network that would make my business more attractive to investors? What elements of the business model could be expanded to improve my company's chances of becoming a market leader? What else could be done to increase the valuation of the enterprise to align it with my expectations? What makes me disagree with the feedback I am receiving? What am I missing? Is it too soon to assign this high a valuation to an enterprise in its early stages? Where can I find data that would support my view or refute it?

Before it was all over, Karen had leveraged her home, and soon she lost it, along with her entire investment, when her company failed because of a lack of capital. She paid an unfortunate personal financial toll. Had Karen opened herself to feedback and coaching she could have promoted the many viable aspects to her enterprise and the outcome may have been different. Her obstinacy, which some read as arrogance and others, more kindly, chalked up to inexperience, brought her down. Karen would not confront the truth.

. . . .

It is a fact of business life that companies fail. In spite of good ideas, burning passion, zealous commitment, and a healthy helping of tenacity, things go wrong. Businesses fail for a variety of reasons, some of which are directly in your control and others that are not.

The U.S. Small Business Administration (SBA) tracks failure rates for small businesses and notes that 50 percent close their doors during the first year of operation. And it normally takes three years for a new small business to achieve solvency. Owners may have to go longer than that before they can draw a steady paycheck.

We are not trying to discourage you. And we know that most entrepreneurs are not easily dissuaded, even in the face of such negative statistics. We know that you are likely to go ahead because you believe in yourself and your idea.

We have seen many businesses cease to exist. Failure is never a pleasant experience for an entrepreneur. And there is never an easy way to deal with the ramifications—personal debt, disrupted relationships, feelings of inadequacy.

If you conducted yourself professionally and ethically, and you gave your all, you can look upon your business "failure" in a positive light, as a learning experience that's worth the price of the education alone. We call this "failing forward." This may be hard to understand at the time. But a business failure does not preclude your trying again. As one entrepreneur said, "Failure offers the chance to try again with better information." At the very least, you will be better prepared the second time around. And like most other things in life, experience is the best teacher. Depending on the specific circumstances, you may be able to solicit advice and help from the same people who helped you in your first venture and perhaps re-approach those who backed you financially.

Our goal with this book is to help improve your chances for success. Understanding common themes around business failures will help you to be better prepared.

Some common themes:

FINANCIAL

Businesses fail because they lack sufficient capital to move forward. In fact, the lack of properly capitalizing your business is the most common reason for failure. Neglecting to plan for your personal financial needs is another key reason. Could you forgo a paycheck for three years and still pay the rent?

EMOTIONAL

You may not have adequately weighed the time commitment and personal sacrifice that being an entrepreneur entails. Or your life circumstances may change: a divorce, an illness, caring for others. These will all impact your ability to sustain an enterprise in the early days. Did you start your own business for the right reasons and understand the extent of the emotional commitment required to see it through rough times?

COLLABORATIVE

Choose your partners wisely. Personal, ethical, and professional differences among partners can directly impact the viability of an enterprise. Your company's integrity is by definition an extension of your own. Are you professionally engaged with a person whose values and integrity mirror yours?

EXTERNAL

A negative change in the economic environment and capital markets can hurt any business, new or mature. Further, global events and political upheaval can also deliver unforeseen challenges. Have you properly planned for a worst-case scenario?

COMPANY AND MARKET SPECIFIC

Do you understand clearly the market and customers for your product? Who will buy it, why, and how much they are willing to pay for it? Do you understand your competitors? Does your business model allow you to create a healthy bottom line? Do you know what your expenses are and have you properly budgeted your costs? Are your margins strong enough to sustain the business? What can go wrong in the market, with your business model, your idea, and your execution?

. . . .

Sheila Schectman, the founder and CEO of Giftcorp, is another story. She has an amazing talent for finding unique and appealing products and a knack for merchandising them. Her company operates in a profitable segment of the gift industry, creating customized gift assortments for corporate customers, event planners, and promotional products groups. For example, one of Sheila's clients is a luxury automobile dealer; to acknowledge its clients and thank them for purchasing its high-end vehicles, the dealer sees that a beautiful gift basket from Giftcorp is sitting on the front seat when they pick up their new cars—and every time their cars are serviced, too.

But in the summer of 2002, it was apparent that there was a problem: During her expansion from a regional to a national presence, Sheila had allowed the cost side of her business to run far ahead of revenues. At the same time, her efforts to raise needed expansion capital had run dry. She faced the very real issue of having to stave off creditors until the Christmas season, the biggest quarter for her business, and her chances of this looked iffy—very iffy. When Sheila met with us, she was wrung out from sleeplessness and stress, but she hadn't given up. She vowed, "There's no way I will let this company fail. Not for everything that I've been through. Not for all of my investors believing in this—and in me. Quitting now is just not an option. I'll do whatever it takes."

We knew what Sheila was made of and that her business plan was fundamentally sound. We added our voices to hers and talked through some of the possibilities together. We asked tough questions: Where can you cut costs? Can you talk to your landlord about reducing the rent? Can you work out a deferred payment schedule with some of your creditors? Can you develop a new sales plan, hire independent reps, and exchange salary for higher commissions? What else can you do to keep the lights on?

Sheila made hard decisions, eliminated her own paycheck right then, and went to bed that night wondering how she could face the future. But the next day she woke up more invigorated; she had a fresh perspective and the will to take action which she described as a shifting of energy. She made the changes we'd discussed and came up with other creative options. Christmas did come for Sheila, and her business has grown at a healthy rate ever since.

We've seen this effect again and again, the sickening feeling of touching bottom, then a surge of new energy that follows when you've faced reality, weighed the alternatives, found a solution that works, and started to carry out that solution.

Sheila's story demonstrates the resourcefulness that springs from tenacity; how just hanging in there affords you the time to digest the information embodied in a defeat, internalize it, and return to your vision as home base, regroup, and move forward again. There's no hiding from the truth. The best

DIGGING DEEPER

Tenacious vs. Obstinate?

Sometimes it's hard to tell whether you are in the righteous throes of saving your manifestly doable business or whether you're butting your head repeatedly into a solid brick wall. Here's how to tell the difference.

Obstinacy looks like this:

- You answer criticism with "Yeah, but," or "You don't understand."
- You interrupt a critic or advisor before that person finishes speaking.
- You often say, "We've tried that already and it didn't work."
- You're afraid of looking bad, so you dig in your heels.
- You press on, regardless of the facts, data, and feedback.

Tenacity, or what we call positive perseverance, looks like this:

- You're vision-driven, not ego-driven.
- You keep an open mind and weigh all the pros and cons.
- You continually re-prioritize and always find the advantage in the disadvantage.
- You incorporate the lessons of failure and learn to turn "no" into "know."

If you would like to explore this important distinction further, see our quiz "Do You Have What It Takes?" on page 194 of the Tool Kit.

course is to face it, learn from it, and exploit it—even when tenacity involves sacrifice.

There will be many times during the building of your business when tenacity is all you have. Customers dwindle, money runs out, investors back down; your partners are depressed and your employees quit to take jobs with more opportunity at the Starbucks down the street. In these moments of truth, you will have to make a go/no go decision at exactly the time when you are emotionally most fragile.

DIGGING DEEPER

Valuation

What It Is

If you decide to raise outside investment dollars (and there will be more about this in the chapter that follows), the valuation of your company becomes a critically important issue. Determined by outside investors, valuation is an estimate of the value of your company. Valuation is based on objective and subjective factors such as the stage of development, the quality of the management team, and upside and growth potential, among others. Although valuation is a highly negotiated and mutually agreed upon number between you and your potential investors, the investors typically hold the upper hand in these negotiations because they hold the cash and it is their money at stake. And, typically, you do not have many alternatives to consider when raising cash to build your business.

Although valuation is expressed in dollars (i.e., $5 million), implying some kind of definitive determining equation, the reality is that valuation is a subjective and arbitrary number. And there is no published database on private-company valuations available as there is for publicly traded stocks. It is very much based on (1) supply and demand (the number and types of deals in the market at any given time and the cash available for investment); and (2) on comparisons, or "benchmarks," relative to companies at a similar stage and in a similar market to yours. Since this knowledge is more readily available to the investor, who is doing the deal, than to the entrepreneur, who is not regularly involved in such transactions, once again the investor has an advantage. It's like selling your house: The buyers ultimately set the price.

Valuation assessments change over time depending on the health of the economy and capital markets and the supply of capital. Some early-stage companies without product, customers, or full management teams were able to command "pre-money" valuations on the order of from $5 to $15 million at the peak of the Internet bubble of the late 1990s. Today, that range would be between $1 and $2 million

(continues)

if the company were lucky enough to find an investor still interested in funding early-stage companies. The key is not to be wedded to any particular number, but to know that valuations can vary dramatically over time depending on the market environment.

What to Know

"Pre-money" valuation is the valuation your investor will assign to your particular enterprise before any outside capital is invested, the somewhat arbitrary number discussed above, based on assessments regarding the size of your target market, the quality of your management team, and the long-term potential of your company.

"Post-money" valuation is what your company will be worth after the infusion of outside capital. Pre-money valuation + cash invested = post-money valuation.

The pre- and post-money numbers are important because they determine how much of your company the outside investor(s) will own after the deal is closed—and how much you, as the company founder, will give up.

Here's an example: Let's assume that before taking outside capital, you and your co-founder each own 50 percent of the stock in your company. If your company is valued at $2 million "pre-money" by your investors and they will invest $1 million, the "post-money" valuation is $3 million. ($2 + $1 = $3). Your investor now owns 33 percent of your company ($1/$3 =33 percent). Your ownership and that of your cofounder are now "diluted" to 66 percent in total, or 33 percent of the stock for each of you. You must weigh the choice of giving up ownership in your company—in this example, a third of it—to attract outside investment. Because the concept of "dilution" often becomes a stumbling block for entrepreneurs, the important question to ask yourself is this: "Do I want 100 percent of a cupcake, or a smaller slice of a very large pie?"

As you create your company and the legal ownership that goes along with it, you will be authorizing and assigning shares in the company to yourself and other owners. You will also be setting aside

(continues)

shares in an "option pool" for incentives for your employees. A key document related to share ownership is called the "cap table," (for capitalization) and it is important that you set it up correctly from the outset. Authorizing and issuing shares, as well as warrants (a right to buy future shares at advantageous prices) if you need to issue them, also factor into dilution and will impact your percentage ownership of the company. Thus, it is very important to track the shares you issue, issue them judiciously, and have the guidance of good legal counsel.

Exit Strategy

Outside investors invest in early-stage companies to receive a significant return on their investment. The endgame for accomplishing this is the "exit strategy"—how the investors will ultimately receive their return. If you do decide to take outside investment, become knowledgeable about the endgame for your company. Will it be a sale to a large public company, or even an IPO (Initial Public Offering)? Be articulate in your discussions with investors about why your company will be attractive to other entities that are likely buyers, and over what time frame you see this happening. Your exit strategy, although an event several years off in the future and subject to much speculation, will play a key role in the amount at which your company is valued today.

Remember

This is an overly simplistic overview of the valuation process, but will help you understand the terminology used in pricing negotiations.

Make sure that when you raise outside capital you engage an attorney experienced in working with venture-funded companies to help you through the maze of legal documents and provide sound advice during the negotiations. An experienced attorney may even help you get the best price for your company because he or she will be working on several deals at a time and have a window into the market on valuations.

Be realistic about your company's value. Many a negotiation has broken down because the entrepreneur held on to a valuation for her

(continues)

company that was unrealistic. Remember, when all is said and done, the true valuation of your company is the price someone else is willing to pay for it.

This is a daunting process, and it would be of benefit to have someone who has gone through this process before as a member of your board.

· · · ·

The entire picture is rarely apparent at the very beginning; it emerges as you build your business. Tenacity is the positive perseverance you need to gut it through while your business is assailed by what the noted economist Joseph Schumpeter called the "forces of creative destruction." Tenacity is one of the essential tools you will use in the months and years ahead. It is particularly important if you decide to raise money from others. In the next chapter, we will look at the different types of funding available to grow your business, which kind may be the most appropriate, and how and where to get it.

· · · ·

WHAT YOU NEED TO KNOW

- When you hit rock bottom, don't deny the problem or your feelings of fear, frustration, and anxiety. Carve out time to fret. It's okay to cry, scream, withdraw into a fetal position, and pull the sheets over your head—for a day. Then get up and face the issues.

- Get help. Find a truth-teller whom you respect, someone who has no financial or emotional investment in the game. Create an ad hoc team of business people you trust. Ask them to a meeting during which you can describe your situation and ask for their advice. There is strength in numbers, and such a meeting can provide positive motivation as well as concrete directions for recovery.
- Listen to understand; not to explain, answer, or defend. Remember, while it's hard to hear criticism of someone or something you love, the truth is your friend.
- Take stock of what you have done and what you are doing well. At times like these there are so many negatives that it is appropriate to balance them with some positives.
- Even if you have made a major error, don't "take yourself to the woodshed." It is easy to berate yourself, but this won't help solve the problem and will only erode your self-image. Acknowledge the mistake, fret if you have to, mine the lessons that are available, revise your plan, and move on.
- Ask yourself the questions required of any enterprise: Is the opportunity really real for both the market and the product? What is our sustainable competitive advantage? Can we be a market leader? Is it worth it to move forward? What are the financial and emotional risks and rewards?
- Do a gut-check. Are you fighting for survival and can you win? Or are you butting your head repeatedly against a stone wall?
- Revisit your vision for renewed inspiration.

CHAPTER 6

Raising Capital

TRANSLATING YOUR VISION
INTO DOLLARS AND SENSE

*The only way not to think about money is to have a
great deal of it.*

Edith Wharton

There's no getting around it. Funding your company is a full-
time objective that's as important as anything you do—product development, marketing, getting customers in the door. Let's
face it, without capital, there won't be a product, let alone a marketing budget. The sources of funding available to you run a long
and dizzying gamut from checking account overdraft to multimillion-dollar stakes by professional investors. And here's something to know: Fifty-five percent of all new businesses are started
with an average of $5,000 from the entrepreneur's own pocket. In
this chapter, we'll look at the many kinds of funding available.

· · · ·

You've already undergone soul searching in making the decision
to take the leap into entrepreneurship. But you're not done yet.

How you fund your business requires more soul searching about the types of funding sources your business is likely to attract. And, just as important, you must be honest about the sources of funding with which you will ultimately be the most comfortable. This is not all black and white. There are important distinctions and nuances to consider when funding a business. For starters, here are three things to think about:

- *Access to Capital:* This is key. Gaining access to funding channels requires that you gain entry into a connected network; this will make your funding search infinitely easier. It will also require that you feel comfortable asking people you know to introduce you to people you *should* know.
- *Funding Choices:* Know what your options are—they can range anywhere from "maxing" out on your credit cards to the elite world of venture-capital funding.
- *Funding Sources:* Who and what type of person or institution is likely to fund your business? This is closely tied to the type of industry you are in, the size of the market opportunity, the rate of growth of the enterprise, its uniqueness, and its ultimate profitability.

When it comes to funding, "Where do I start?" is the most frequently asked question we hear from budding entrepreneurs. There are lots of choices, and given the coverage by the business media devoted to "venture capital," most entrepreneurs want to run right there. But like Dorothy in the *Wizard of Oz*, your best bet is to begin by looking in your own backyard. Although we profile many entrepreneurs in this book who raised sizeable sums of money, research shows that, surprisingly, most new businesses are started with the entrepreneur's personal savings, on average from $5,000 to $10,000. It may not make sense to go right out of the starting gate looking for a lot of money. Or, as you grow and establish your business, the funding sources may want to talk to you.

To get a sense of what type of funding is most appropriate for your company, begin by determining the type of business and the potential size of the business you hope to build, and the cash needs required to achieve your ultimate goal. It may be helpful to refer back to the work you did in the exercises from the Tool Kit.

Nobody can predict the future, but you can imagine the kind and size of business that fits your dream. Do you want to have a one-person company in your own home that gives you the flexibility to set your own schedule; a ten-person firm on Main Street where you know all your employees and customers by name; or a national company with hundreds of people on the payroll and a reputation as an industry innovator? Or, thinking even bigger, do you want a global enterprise of 30,000 employees and your picture on the cover of *Fortune Magazine*?

To further help visualize the type of company you are setting out to build, write a press release about where your company will be five years from now; think about the size, scope, type of operation, and the accomplishment the press release will be celebrating. This will help you place your company on the continuum of financing options.

Now, with the aid of the information from both your passion and vision exercises and the mock press release, the world of funding follows the same spectrum as the size of your intended business. We call this spectrum the "funding food chain." (See

Figure 6.1.) The smaller your business, the more you will have
to rely on your own money and personal access to credit, "bootstrapping" (creative ways to stretch your resources), and help
from your friends and family.

The bigger your envisioned business, the more advanced your
needs will be along the food chain. It becomes more realistic to
think about getting money from banks or outside private equity
sources such as professional angel investors, venture capitalists,
strategic investors, or even all of these. But don't ignore bootstrapping at any level. When the capital markets dry up, no matter how large a company you have, bootstrapping and cash con-
servation must be top priorities.

So, with that as a beginning, here's a brief rundown of your
options on the food chain:

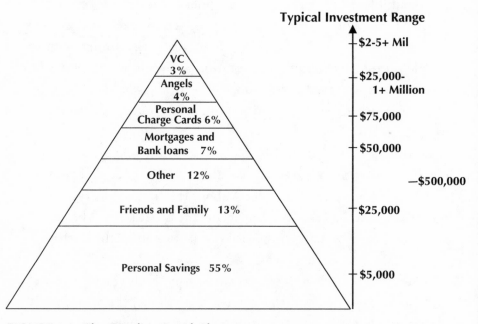

FIGURE 6.1   The Funding Food Chain
Source: Census Bureau data, *Inc Magazine,* 8Wings

KINDS OF FINANCING

Your own internal resources: These can begin with a second mortgage on your home, credit card debt, the support of a spouse or partner, or the sometimes liberating event of being laid off from a corporation and given a six-month severance package that finally affords you the freedom to pursue your dream of starting a business. *Most new businesses are funded through internal resources.*

Bootstrapping: This is where your creativity and ingenuity come into play. How successful you can be at bootstrapping will depend on the cash flow needs of your business. Bootstrapping includes such things as bartering your services for those of another vendor, hiring part-time help, sharing office space, buying used equipment, stretching out vendor payments, issuing equity in your company in lieu of cash to key service providers, and any other ways that you can imagine. And although bootstrapping entails buying on the cheap and doing more with less, it really is more about mindset and overall discipline in judiciously conserving capital and not spending before you need to.

Family and friends: This is different than relying on a spouse's paycheck for survival. You will be asking family and friends to fund your business directly; in exchange, you will give them an instrument tied to the growth of your business. Raising a so-called "family and friends" investment moves you one step closer to the big leagues because it is a formal transaction in which you will be issuing stock or some form of a debt instrument in exchange for their cash. Be very cognizant of your family's financial situation. If this is money they cannot afford to lose, do not ask or expect them to invest in your business. If they are well heeled, be aware of the expectations and obligations—as well as the limitations. If your family Thanksgivings already resemble a Woody Allen movie, think twice before further complicating already complex relationships because now there is a monetary obligation to fulfill.

Microlending programs: There are various programs where a lending institution has lowered minimum requirements and will lend small amounts, sometimes as little as $250, to help get small businesses off the ground. These programs are often targeted at specific objectives, such as bringing more jobs into a community, or helping underrepresented entrepreneurs, including women, to have a better shot at starting a company. It may take some digging on your part to uncover these programs.

Bank debt and commercial loans: These avenues are typically closed to early-stage entrepreneurs; banks will usually lend only to companies that can support a debt burden with existing cash flow, which tends to be nonexistent in a new venture. They might lend to you if you have an asset, such as business equipment or your own home, that can be used as collateral to back up a loan. This again can be a luxury for most early-stage companies. Some banks have special programs sponsored by the Small Business Administration (SBA) that waive some of these requirements.

DIGGING DEEPER

How Banks Lend Money

Because banks lend out depositors' funds to make their money, they cannot take risks with those funds. In extending loans, bankers follow what's called the "five C's" of lending:

- Character—Does the borrower have a strong credit history and a reputation as a person of character and integrity?
- Capacity—Does the borrower demonstrate sufficient cash flow from the business, from personal sources, or from a combination

(continues)

of the two to make the principal and interest payments over the life of the loan?

- Capital—does the borrower's business reflect a solid net worth (i.e., excess of assets over liabilities) that will cushion unexpected fluctuations in business conditions?
- Conditions—How will current conditions in the economy impact the borrower's business, and hence her ability to repay the loan?
- Collateral—Does the borrower have a source of collateral, a tangible and liquid asset that can be pledged to repay the loan in the event cash flow sources become insufficient?

The Small Business Administration (SBA) does offer loans through designated banks specifically for early-stage companies that have minimal revenues. This is a valid source for entrepreneurs to use in funding start-up working capital needs. (For more information on the government's SBA program, see the SBA's Online Women's Business Center at www.onlinewbc.gov). But, unless you're able to get an SBA loan or find some other special bank program, don't be surprised if you are repeatedly turned down.

Angel investors: Angel investment falls into the category of private equity. Angels are wealthy individuals who invest their own capital in early-stage companies. This is a growing source of capital that in total actually exceeds the dollar amounts the better-known venture capitalists provide to early-stage companies.

Venture capital: Surprisingly, although this sector is clearly the most visible, it provides the smallest amount of total funding to early-stage companies. Because venture capitalists (VCs) tend to invest in companies operating in large markets and requiring millions of dollars to grow, many leading VC firms have backed well-known success stories, the reason they are so highly visible. And that is why entrepreneurs want to run right to a VC firm when they need money. Yet you have the lowest odds of success, as VCs provide only 3 percent of the total funding on the food chain. In

2001, only 6 percent of that total went to firms led by women, although that number is increasing.

See the Digging Deeper below for further discussion about why women have a harder time raising capital.

Strategic investment: These are large corporate investors who invest in your company to help you develop a product or technology that would be useful to them as part of their strategic direction, or a key supplier that would benefit from your success.

DIGGING DEEPER

Why do women have a different ability and experience when raising capital? We have found that there is no one factor but a spectrum of issues that impact women's ability and experience when going out to raise money:

- No historical context, role models, or mentors.
- No guidebooks or guidelines.
- The process is an old boys' network.
- The vast majority of deals are funded by referral through established networks.
- Investors believe myths about women and the types of businesses they start; that is, small businesses, or what are called "lifestyle" businesses that enable one to work part time and stay at home.
- Women are socialized differently from men and have a lower comfort zone when it comes to talking about their own capabilities, expertise, and accomplishments.
- There is often a difference in style and presentation skills.
- Women internalize criticism; men deflect it. Securing funding is a highly critical process.
- Women bring a different perspective to the negotiating table.
- Less than 10 percent of venture capital partners are women; an estimated 5 percent of angel investors are women.

A BOOTSTRAPPING AND ANGEL-FUNDING STORY

Pat Meisner, CEO of Red Tail Solutions, likes to order in Thai food for lunch with her entire company, all four of them, in their large one-room office inside an old building in western Massachusetts. The company Pat formed with her business partner, Jeff Franklin, is a software service that makes it possible and easy for small companies to transact business electronically with jumbo-sized customers.

If you're a small vendor selling to a retail giant like Wal-Mart, you must be able to trade with them electronically: Purchase orders, invoices, shipping instructions—all have to go over the Internet, or the company's own private trading network. A business the size of Wal-Mart may have 1,500 stores across the country, and when they order goods from a vendor there might be hundreds of line items going to stores in different shipping locations. Companies of this magnitude also want to be able to pull up those orders into their own business forms. For smaller companies, it's typically done over a fax machine, but they are being pushed to do it all electronically—no paper. It's a complex and pricey process to set up a compatible hardware and software system, align it, test it, train people, and then get it running. Red Tail provides the vendor companies with an easy-to-use software package that can be self-installed over the Internet. Then Red Tail handles the electronic transformation of orders and information in both directions. The company believes there is a sizeable market opportunity for its software, and that it is cheaper and more efficient to use than other products in the market. Armed with introductions from some of the company's advisors, Red Tail decided to go out and raise venture capital.

"Jeff came up with the technical solution and I came up with how you could build a business around it. So I've been the one on the business side just figuring out how to get it funded, keep it going, keep it growing, how to weather probably the most brutal market period we've ever had."

Pat recalled how hard it was to get funding:

Red Tail Solutions was incorporated in early 2000, about a year into the whole dot-com and Internet explosion. We thought, "Everything is getting funded." You didn't even need a complete business plan back then. Still, we took a very systematic, professional approach to putting a well-developed business plan in place. And we thought surely if we go out with this, it's going to be simple to get funding.

We weren't a dot-com company but we used many of the buzz words that were used at that time, hoping to catch the wave. What we failed to notice was that the Internet wave had crested and was already starting to curl over and crash. Investors had begun to recognize that there were some fatal flaws in many of those Internet businesses. It was probably our fault that we wasted so much time that first twelve months, and it was a rude awakening when it became clear that it was not going to be an easy proposition to get money from venture people.

So Pat anted up $125,000 of her own money, estimating that this seed money would keep their infant company going while she and her partner hunkered down and focused on their prospective customers' needs and got a product out as quickly as possible.

One of my philosophies is to just do it and learn where the weak parts are, or the wrong assumptions, and make your corrections.

So we got the software out very early. And, as a result, we got our first customer and a lot of good customer feedback and made a lot of enhancements to our product as we went along. And we thought, "Now surely we'd get funding," so we went out again but found that the bar for obtaining funding had been raised again. We were told, "It's nice that you have a product and one customer, but now we need to see revenues and we need to see traction."

That became the new catch phrase, "You've got to get some traction." And I said, "What is traction?" And I was told it was like a snowball rolling down a mountain, increasing in diameter with every foot. Translated, that means having more than one customer. And once you get one, you better be on to your second, your third, fourth, and so on.

At that point, Pat and Jeff realized that they were probably not going to get venture funding, but to keep their business running they still needed more seed money than they could come up with personally. Then that summer, Pat read a story in the *Boston Globe* about a group of angel investors who invest in women-run businesses. She made a call, and got on the schedule to meet with this group. A few months later, Pat presented her business plan to the Center for Women & Enterprise, and we were in the audience that day. After that meeting, Kathy Elliott, one of the 8Wings partners, worked closely with Pat to help her refine her business model. Pat worked hard, took in a lot of feedback, and continued to push her company along. Several months later, having experienced firsthand Pat's determination and focus, and how judicious she was in spending her company's capital, Kathy encouraged 8Wings to participate in the company's first round of financing, an angel round. Along with other angels, we have since participated in a second round.

Pat's company is moving forward now.

People laugh when we tell them what our "burn rate" is, the monthly cost of running the business, because we're very frugal. [And note that the burn rate is an important number for investors because it tells them how long a company can survive on the cash they have on hand.] When there were just two of us, our burn rate was about $15,000 a month for everything. We added a third person and we work with a few extra part-time people now, so our burn rate now is about $25,000 a month. When it looked as if we were running out of cash, we all took pay cuts, which were already sort of token salaries, far below fair market. And we're still on the pay cuts until we can secure our next round of funding. We don't buy anything until after we need it. And I think that our frugality was a very powerful signal to our current investors. They saw how committed we were and how much promise we have given the opportunity. We've been very conservative with our spending, all the while continuing to make progress.

Red Tail is indeed gaining traction as we write this; it has more than thirty-five customers and a proven product. The company is in the throes of pursuing venture funding again so that it can build a sales team and capitalize on its current sales momentum.

As Pat reflected, "Had I continued to plug along as we were going without our angels, I don't think we would be here to tell about it. Those angels are very smart. They mentored us. They made connections for us. If I'd chosen just some random high-wealth individuals I'm sure we would have burned through the cash right away because we wouldn't have gotten the ongoing and continuing connections that are needed to grow our business."

DIGGING DEEPER

Creative Ways to Stretch Your Dollar—Bootstrapping

The origin of the word "bootstrapping" dates back to the 1800s. Bootstraps were small leather loops sewn into boots to help pull them on. "To pull oneself up by the bootstraps" has meant to succeed by one's own efforts without outside help.

In the same sense, bootstrapping a company has come to mean growing a company by internal means without the help of outside financing. As Jaimee Wolf of Xicat says, "It's stretch the cash as long as possible." It's doing more with less, becoming creative about the methods of bringing cash in the door, and adopting a disciplined attitude toward your cash management.

Here's a brief outline of major expense items that you can minimize with a creative and disciplined approach:

- *Office space*: Beg, borrow, barter, or steal. Look for creative opportunities to share space, locate undervalued space, or piggyback on the excess space of existing companies. And it is important in the early stages to forego rental expense altogether and continue to work from the second bedroom or kitchen table until you are ready to take off. For example, Pat negotiated a reduced rent for being the first tenant in a newly rehabbed office building.
- *Services:* Barter for services. Figure out what you bring to the table and how you can horse trade for what you need. Again, Red Tail used Jeff's technical expertise to reduce rent further when Jeff installed new high-speed Internet lines in the building for all tenants to share. And be creative. Services for trade can run the gamut from PR and marketing to legal and accounting.
- *Personnel:* Stay flexible and hire contract personnel and part-timers to minimize fixed cost (health insurance and associated benefits). Use cheaper sources of labor where possible, such as graduate students. And be stingy with lofty titles up front; keep your organization flat and lean.

(*continues*)

- *Equipment:* eBay is the way. Scour the secondhand market for capital equipment and office furniture. Red Tail acquired a sophisticated bar code printer on eBay for pennies on the dollar, and it has allowed them to offer a new product line to customers.
- *Cheap capital:* Don't be afraid to take advantage of zero-interest-rate credit cards and keep rolling them as teaser rates expire. Second, your house may represent a source of hidden capital. Borrowing against your home is a tax-advantaged vehicle. Caution is needed, however, so you don't overleverage. We do not advise borrowing from 401-Ks or retirement plans. You'll pay a heavy tax penalty and lose the significant advantage of tax-deferred investment growth.
- *Freebies:* Take advantage of free trials, such as one-month subscriptions to Internet services or research sources.
- *Get money in the door:* Structure your product's pricing so that you get some of your revenues up front, even if it means offering a discount. Charge an installation fee or up-front consulting fee for implementation.

Bootstrapping can be a positive discipline. The dot-coms that blew $20 million on branding and advertising with nothing to show for it could have benefited from a bootstrapping mentality. Bootstrapping brings a systematic decisionmaking perspective that can inject discipline into how you spend or conserve your scarce capital. It can provide you with an opportunity to grow in a controlled manner as you prove your business model; it also can help you increase the value of your company before you take in the first outside investment dollar by moving you that much ahead.

But beware: Bootstrapping can foster a penny-wise, pound-foolish operating mentality. It may place artificial constraints on your company's growth. It can also lead to challenging relationships with vendors as you try to stretch payment cycles.

TURNED DOWN BY THE BANKS

Sheila Schectman, the CEO of Giftcorp, introduced in the last chapter, vividly remembers twenty-one years ago when she went to six banks to finance her first company and was turned down by all six of them: "I was called a 'mere housewife'— even though I had already put $100,000 into the company and the loan I sought would have been collateralized. I finally ended up with an SBA loan, which in the early 1980s hovered at 21.5 percent interest. That was expensive money and I had to personally sign for everything, but my company made it through all that. It is still difficult for women to get a bank loan for a new business."

She financed Giftcorp with her own money for the first seven years; then she decided to go national and needed to seek outside funding:

> For our first round of funding, we were looking to raise $5 million and there was a VC who wanted to put in the whole piece. And they also wanted control of the company. I'm not a control freak, but I'm unwilling to have somebody, just because they have money, come in, run a company, and control it. To me, that is the biggest danger. There are a lot of good VCs out there, but typically for smaller companies I think women with great ideas are better off raising angel money. And that's what I did. I eventually raised less than the initial $5 million I was looking for, but I have investors I am more comfortable with.

Sheila recalled the time she first met with and was questioned by Connie Duckworth, another 8Wings partner, about her financial plans.

I know it sounds idiotic, but when Connie asked me sound yet sophisticated questions, I didn't know what she was talking about. She took the time to explain the jargon, which is really half the game. I've learned a great deal since then and continue to benefit from the Wings' input.

You have to put ego aside when raising money. You've got to be able to listen and to respond to the questions asked. When you first start pitching to investors I think that beginning entrepreneurs should bring a financial person with them to a presentation. It's great to have support as well as an extra pair of eyes and ears to help watch the body language and read between the lines. You shouldn't feel that you have to know everything, and bringing a business advisor to a presentation is far better than trying to hobble through it yourself.

Although it may not be a requirement that you know every financial detail, the more you know the better when speaking to angels and VCs. More important, you *must* know the key fundamentals of your company, the industry you are operating in, your distribution channels, and your competition.

FAMILY AND FRIENDS, ANGELS AND VCs — THE FULL SPECTRUM

Although most entrepreneurs have a good fix on the type of business they want to start, Janet Kraus and her business partner, Kathy Sherbrooke, knew that they wanted to start a service business with the capacity to become large and national. They had a vision, they just didn't have the specific business in mind. So they started a deliberate process to figure out what that business would be:

Kathy and I wanted to start a company that solved a really big market need. We wanted the corporate culture to be awesome, located in a place where people would love working. We wanted a company that sold information and services as opposed to products. A company that could be successful at a midsize or a really large size. A company that took advantage of what we thought was our strength as individuals, which was putting people in contact with other people and things or services or information that they need. We decided that we wanted to build a service company that would improve the efficiency of our clients' employees and also leverage and help our clients' brands get better by increasing customer loyalty. We knew starting out that we wanted to build a company big enough to attract venture funding.

We interviewed thousands of people who represented our target market and asked them what their personal needs were, what their pains were, would they pay to solve the pain.

Sorting through the interviews, they concluded that, with the exception of grocery shopping, there was little consensus within this group concerning the top priorities on their to-do lists.

Their interview subjects were vague and said, "I have a million things to do. I just need someone to help me get stuff done." Janet and Kathy recognized this as the "big" problem their business could tackle: "Wow, how do we solve a problem that's this big? What does that even consist of? What are we talking about? Is it buying gifts? Is it planning parties? Is it getting a dog walker?"

Janet figured that she had enough in her savings account to last her eighteen months if she lived modestly. Then she and Kathy quit their jobs and researched "big trends," finally honing in on a segment of the population they described as "time-starved professionals."

So, Kathy and Janet decided to help "time-starved professionals" get "stuff done" by creating a concierge service that could help these people with almost anything they could articulate, and they'd do it 24/7. They called their brainchild "Circles" (to connote running around in circles). Much to their credit, they wisely eschewed the knee-jerk advice—popular during the Internet boom—that they put their service on the Web and sell directly to consumers. Instead, Janet and Kathy decided to market their services directly to large corporations that in effect would bundle large volumes of customers for them—their employees—by making their concierge service part of an employee benefit package. Circles also offered their services to large corporations who would in turn offer Circles' products to their own customers to help retain their business. The attraction for the corporate clients of Circles' was the opportunity to enhance their own bottom lines by either improving the efficiency of their employees or by helping to improve customer loyalty.

Circles targets airlines and credit card companies that would offer these services as a perk to their frequent fliers and gold- and platinum-grade card-holders. They also identify human resource executives at large corporations who would use Circles as a benefit for their employees and, at the same time, benefit by drastically reducing the time each day most workers spend attending to personal chores (on average, three hours).

In so doing, Circles does what no other company has done before: A customer sends his or her "to do list" online and Circles handles the requests through a call center made up of two hundred "personal assistants" and a virtual network of service providers. Each ultimate customer is made to feel that he or she has a personal concierge to call upon. Circles can do almost anything—from picking up dry cleaning and arranging for someone to walk the dog to locating night-vision goggles or putting together a surprise fiftieth birthday party. While millions of people now use this service, most have never heard of Circles because the company "private labels" its services under the names of their large corporate clients.

Comfortable in her spacious and well-lit office, Janet thought back to the early days when she and Kathy were selling air: "When we first started Circles, there was no concierge industry. We were the first to market and define the industry. I say this because a lot of people didn't know what we were talking about when we first began to develop it."

Although their path to starting the company was not the typical one, once they were on their way, their story became a textbook example of how to fund a business.

Janet and Kathy started Circles with the financial resources available to them: about $30,000 in their own combined credit card debt, an often-used initial source of capital for entrepreneurs. They drafted a business plan, then raised $400,000 from friends and family; they formalized this transaction not as a loan but as an equity investment, a responsibility they took seriously, complete with professionally drafted documents. Equity is a piece of ownership in a company. In exchange for cash, the investor receives a percentage of the business. If the business fails, the equity investors lose their money. As Janet recounts:

I think the most important thing about a "family and friends" type of investment is to make it really clear to them that they could lose it all. If you aren't close enough to them to say, "If you lost $50,000, would you be okay?" then don't take the money.

You also have to be very clear about what your family and friends' financial capabilities really are. Even if everyone understands the conditions, you still have to look them in the eye at holidays and every weekend when they ask how the business is going. And you have to respond, even if you're not in the mood to talk about it.

For Janet and Kathy, fear of Thanksgiving dinner came home to roost nine months after taking on the initial "family and friends" round of financing; they realized that their new business would be out of cash in about three months' time and they had not yet gained traction in the corporate market. "We were down to about $40,000 of the $400,000. We'd sent back the water cooler, given up two-thirds of our space, and were thinking about moving back into my house and wiring it up for our computers. The situation was truly dire. And then, of course, we had to present to our investors, which at this point are our best friends and blood relatives."

Janet and Kathy told their investors that their investment was headed down the tubes and that they could either close up shop and return the pitiful remains of the seed money or they could keep moving forward. But to do that, they would need more financing. One of their investors requested more information about the corporate market Kathy and Janet had identified and asked how they planned to sell to these clients, how many clients they thought they could sell within the next three months, and whether three months' worth of additional financing would be "crossing the chasm" to solvency.

Janet and Kathy said that it would and they laid out their plan. Janet continued the story: "So our investors stepped up and gave us a $100,000 bridge loan that we had to sign for personally to tide us over. This bridge loan would convert to equity if we got through the hole. But if we didn't, we each owed another $50,000. We took the money and we signed away our future. And we crossed that chasm. We got three or four corporate clients over the next couple months that brought in enough revenue to cover our expenses, and we were back in business."

As the company grew and needed more capital to continue to grow even more, Janet and Kathy decided that it was time to raise capital from angel investors. Nearly eighteen months after launching Circles, they raised $1.6 million in angel money. It was not easy to raise such funding, but the company had proved the soundness of its business model, had put together a credible and competent management team, and had shown it had the ability to grow into a fairly large-sized company—all necessary criteria to bring in angel investors:

> The first five years we were a concierge company, more in the traditional sense of the word. As we go from the first five years toward ten years, we define ourselves as a loyalty management solutions company. This is a broader market space, a larger market, with attractive economic characteristics. We are all about connecting our clients to their customers and their employees in unique ways that help create bonds of loyalty and drive the bottom line for our clients. Our clients know that they can turn to us with problems, and that we will solve them. That's the value proposition of our company.

By this time, Circles had grown to more than several million dollars in revenues. Pursuing venture capital was the next logical step in their funding evolution. Circles had evolved and grown to the point where it needed larger sums of capital to take advantage of the market opportunity. It wasn't easy finding the right venture firm who understood the opportunity, but the company successfully raised two venture rounds totaling $26 million. Circles is solidly profitable and poised to make acquisitions in the industry to cement their market dominance.

MORE ABOUT ANGEL INVESTORS AND VENTURE CAPITALISTS

For new businesses that appear to have a distinct upside growth potential and a defined path to profitability, angels and venture capitalists are an important source of financing. But these professional investors find only a small percentage of new businesses to be an attractive investment.

The original meaning of the term "angel" came into being in the 1920s when it was used to describe "an early backer of Broadway plays." Broadway plays were high-risk ventures, and the angels who backed them were well-heeled individuals who wanted the status and fun of buying into a theatrical production.

Now "angel" has been re-coined to define wealthy individuals who invest in early-stage start-up companies. Venture capitalists (VCs) are in a similar game as angels, but with different interests and different rules. Although some angels act like VCs and vise versa, the accepted distinction is this: Angels invest their own money. A VC invests other peoples' money. Along with a VC's role comes very strict fiduciary responsibilities and promises to their investors about the management of their portfolios and the resulting returns.

Accordingly, VCs invest in businesses that they determine will grow fast enough and become big enough for the company to be sold. In this way, the VCs can recoup their investment and make the significant returns their clients have hired them for, typically within a five-year time frame. VC firms have strict criteria for their investments, such as the stage of the company they will invest in (i.e., early or later stage), and the industry the company is in (i.e., consumer versus technology, software versus health care). And VCs will typically want from 25 percent to 40 percent ownership of your business and eventual control of the board. That's an important consideration, because VCs can influence the board to fire and replace the founder if they decide it's in the best interest of their investment to do so. (This is explored in more detail in Chapter 9, "Life After the Survival Stage.") Never mind that this company is your passion, your vision, your baby!

By contrast, angels will exert less control over you, although they will expect to have some input as well as a stake in your company, generally speaking from 10 to 30 percent, in exchange for their investment. And, due to the riskiness of early-stage businesses, they will be looking for a return on their investment higher than they might expect from buying stock in a publicly traded company. They no longer operate like earlier angels who backed Broadway plays for the love of theater alone; today's angels expect sizeable returns on their investment. But they won't want a controlling stake in the company, and they may or may not require a board seat. If you do give them an early board seat, you can replace them as your company grows. Angels understand that recasting the board is of ultimate benefit to the company. As you grow and further refine your strategic direction, you have a better sense of the type of individual you want to recruit for your board as well as in what areas you need strategic advice and input.

Most significantly, angels want to get involved with other people's businesses because they enjoy building companies and feel they can contribute significant value in doing so. They don't want to run your company, but they are energized and gratified by helping you grow your company and by making their investment a successful one.

In addition to bringing money to the table, we recommend that you look for the type of angel, a person or group, who can contribute expertise to your entrepreneurial effort: industry knowledge and operating expertise or skills that you may lack. We have an expression, "All money is not the same color green." Indeed, the greenest money offers value added: the support of sophisticated professionals who have industry expertise or who have worked in a field related to yours. Many angels have started and sold successful companies themselves. They like to invest in the industry they operated in and know a lot about. They have contacts they can share with you, and these dream angels will cut you some slack if you miss a milestone— for a good reason—because some have been there themselves as entrepreneurs. They will often develop a personal interest in how your business fares because they have come to know and believe in you. These are the kinds of people you'd love to have on your advisory board and have a stake in your company because they help you build and fuel your business.

We have not spent a lot of time in this book discussing venture capital. It is a highly visible source of funding, but provides only a small percentage of the total financing pie for early-stage companies. And 99 percent of the time, VCs will meet only with entrepreneurs who are introduced to them by some trusted member of their business network. If you believe your business is a candidate for venture funding, try to get an introduction directly to a VC through your attorney or accountant, one of your advisors, or an entrepreneur whose company was funded directly by the venture firm.

STRATEGIC INVESTMENT

Strategic investors are outside corporate/business investors who perceive that your company has assets or innovative technology that will enhance their strategy. This type of investment is not just limited to the VC arms of technology companies that became popular during the Internet bubble (now many are folding). This mode of investing has been around for decades and can take the form of a direct equity investment or customer-funded development for your new product.

A strategic partner may be looking at your company as a window into a new technology or an innovative management team. From your perspective, you are interested in what such a partner can bring to the table for your company in terms of validating your technology, opening a new channel of distribution, or providing cash to grow your company.

The positives of this relationship are numerous; this could represent a source of capital that, depending on the deal, could be structured without diluting your equity stake. Just as important, this type of investor can be your first customer, as well as provide development expertise or access to an already established distribution channel. This relationship automatically lends credibility to your company, and it could provide your future exit strategy.

You should be aware that this type of investment can often represent a double-edged sword. You should be highly cognizant of the potential for conflict. Avoid giving a potential strategic partner exclusivity in using your product, or right of first refusal to an outside acquisition offer. How you structure your agreement in this regard may preclude other large entities from taking an interest in you. Make sure it does not compete with or threaten in any way your relationships with current and potential customers. Typically, strategic investors are large corporations, and because of the nature of the relationship, watch out that you don't allow them to become too influential in directing your company's strategy.

NETWORKING IS THE KEY

The bottom line is that whether you decide to pursue angel funding, venture capital, or both, the search for investment capital is done almost exclusively through networking. Pat Meisner of Red Tail was lucky when she happened upon that article in the *Boston Globe* about angel investors who support women-led companies. That was serendipity; but if she hadn't made the call and followed up to secure a meeting, it might have taken her much longer to find funding, if ever.

Janet Kraus of Circles was new to Boston when she and her partner began their start-up, and she built her network of friends and associates slowly: "I had conversations with people two years before I ever asked them for money. And I put together a spreadsheet that was all about methodically managing a network."

The matrix Janet developed as a way of identifying and linking up possible investors is a wonder of network methodology. On the left-hand side of her spreadsheet, she listed everyone she knew who might possibly be interested in investing. Across the top ran columns with headings such as *How I Know Them, Why I Think They Might Be Interested in Investing, What They've*

Done Before, How Much I Think They Might Be Interested in Investing, Why I Think That, and *Who Else They Know.*

"The spreadsheet I developed was hundreds of people long and ten columns wide, and it wasn't just a database of names, addresses, and phone numbers. This was a much more visual schematic that I could really work with. I'd run my finger across the line that showed Jane Doe knows this person, this person, this person, this person, and this person. I can get to Jane through this person and I can go from Jane to these people. This is how I codified networking to raise angel money."

It's been said that bringing angels to the table is like herding cats.

Angels all come with different perspectives on why they're investing. And it's important to know which of those points of view is most compatible with your style. Before the commitment is made, you will want angels to ask active, engaged questions about your business. You can usually tell from their questions where their interests lie, whether their motivations are similar to yours, whether they are going to be so intrusive they would drive you crazy in the future. And all investors will want to know a great deal about your financial plan. You should be able to provide prospective investors with all the information they need to feel comfortable about investing in you. *You* can and should be direct as well. Ask them what their investment philosophy and guidelines are. You should ask to talk to some of the entrepreneurs running other companies they have funded, both currently and in the past. It may be hard to remember at times that this relationship is a two-way street. If the chemistry is wrong, it could be the most expensive money you ever raise.

· · · ·

DIGGING DEEPER

Networking Insights

- Debunk the isolationist myth—the entrepreneur as "rugged individualist." Successful entrepreneurs are consummate networkers who know that relationship building is the essential link to capital, employees, strategic alliance partners, and all who contribute to their future success.
- Circulate, get out, and get connected. Identify the venues where prospective contacts gather—and go there. Alumni groups, trade organizations, industry councils—all are great "connecting" spots.
- Many organizations are interested in new and motivating speakers. Develop strong presentation skills and offer yourself as an authority in your industry.
- Build relationships before you need them—when the time arrives to ask for help, your network will be waiting.
- Don't be afraid to ask friends, family members, colleagues, former teachers, past bosses, and peers for introductions—and remember to return the value to them in some way.
- You may be thinking, "Why would anyone want to help me?" Approaching people because of their knowledge and expertise is a form of flattery of the highest order. People like to be recognized for their accomplishments, and you would be surprised by how generous most individuals can be.
- Understand the "rule of reciprocity." Networking is about forging relationships, not completing transactions. Recognize your network, be thoughtful in showing your appreciation, and make yourself available when they call on you. Remember, it's a two-way street.
- Don't overstep or wear out your welcome—know what you want from a contact beforehand and respect his or her time.
- Wisdom, knowledge, and business savvy come in many forms; don't eschew or pass over what comes in a simple form. Also, never underestimate the insights of the devil's advocate.
- Learn to listen, but remember that the ultimate decision is your responsibility.

Raising outside capital is a grueling, full-time endeavor. Robin Chase of Zipcar likens it to pushing an elephant through a door jamb: "It's possible, but it takes brute physical force." To save yourself time and frustration, determine at the outset whether your company is the type and potential size suitable for outside investors; then determine how much money you will need to raise. This will entail creating a detailed business plan showing how big your business will be in six months, twelve months, two years; and estimating how much it will cost to get there. Depending on the funding environment, try to raise as much as six months of capital—and a cushion—to meet your plan. One of the classic mistakes entrepreneurs make is not asking for enough money to allow them to reach a cash-positive position.

Preparation is a big part of raising outside capital. Target your list of potential funders, and do not waste time going to those who are unlikely to fund you. Make sure you have all the documents needed. To help you get started, we have included outlines of some of the basic presentation materials in the Tool Kit—your executive summary, business plan, Power Point presentation for investor meetings, and a road map for tapping into the investment world. Solicit advice from someone who has gone through this process, and ask your contacts for samples of these documents that they think are especially good.

DIGGING DEEPER

The Five Things Not *to Say to an Investor*

1. *"We have no competition."* Every company has competition and it can come in many forms. Saying you don't have any shows that you are naïve and that you will be unprepared for competi-

(*continues*)

tive challenges. Focus instead on the "value proposition" of your product. Outline how it solves a customer's "point of pain" or saves them significant money.

2. *"This is an a $80 billion market!"* Yes, the total may be. Industries such as computer software or health care are gigantic. But *your company* will be addressing a much smaller subsegment of the total market. This speaks to focus; you need to target the most appropriate and much narrower segment of the overall market and define it as such. Otherwise, you diminish your chances of getting investment because no one will invest in you to help you figure out what your market truly is. Know precisely who your ultimate customers are and how they make decisions.

3. *"Even if we get just 1 percent of the market, we'll be an $X-million company."* Investors invest in market leaders, not also-rans. And who will have the other 99 percent of the market? Build your revenue model from the bottom up by realistic assessments based on customer acquisition, not by assuming you'll get a small and insignificant share of the total market.

4. *"Yeah, but . . . ."* Push-back and defensiveness toward an investor's question is a sure way to find yourself in perpetual bootstrapping mode.

5. *"We have talked with General Electric, Cisco, and General Motors, and they are all interested in using our product."* Unless you have letters of intent or memorandums of understanding from companies of this stature, you instantly diminish your credibility by making such boastful claims. And you have presented a warning flag of an unintended sort. Companies this large usually take a long time to make decisions about buying new products. A sophisticated investor will read into client names of this magnitude as having very long sales cycles.

As you figure out how you're going to finance your business, you should also have a financial plan for the other parts of your life: food, shelter, electricity. There's been much talk about mortgaging homes and running up credit card debt, but at the end of the day you've got to make money for the business to go forward and for you to live.

Money pressures can be killers, and when you're trying to build a business while worrying about finding the money to pay your car loan your ability to think expansively is hindered. Starting a business takes time, and being properly capitalized *personally* out of the gate will help you focus your energy where you need it most. So plan your new and visionary future through an integrated game plan for living your life *and* building your business.

· · · ·

As you go out into the world to pitch your story, you'll be getting constant feedback about your business. You'll learn what flies, what bombs, what captivates, what to do with blank looks, terrible advice, and new ideas that you've never considered before. Being able to hear feedback, both positive and negative, and to process it so that you can use it to your advantage, is key to your future success.

In the next chapter we will talk about focus, feedback, and flexibility; they are critical during this whole frustrating process of raising capital, but you'll also want to incorporate them as you put your newfound financing to work.

WHAT YOU NEED TO KNOW

- Soul search up front before you start the funding process to determine what types of funding your business is likely to attract and what type of investor you will feel comfortable with.
- Become familiar with and understand the vocabulary used in the funding process. The more you know about

the different kinds of funding sources that are realistic for your business, the more professional and credible you will appear to outsiders. During the funding search, perception becomes reality.

- Explore within yourself whether you are comfortable giving up an equity stake in your company to an outside party. Don't wait until the eleventh hour and realize that you can't or don't want to.

- Be prepared for a difficult and time-consuming process. Fundraising is networking to the max, and will become your full-time job. It takes enormous time, effort, and creativity, and always takes longer than you think.

- Think about starting a business with a partner, as some of the entrepreneurs mentioned in this chapter have done. One of you can focus on finding outside capital; the other can mind the store and build and grow the company.

- Understand that all money is not the same color green. The most desirable investors will do more for you than just write a check; they will add real operating and strategic input, perspective, and value to your business.

- The larger the investment, the more strings there will be attached to it, and the more onerous and stringent the requirements for communication and performance will be. Understand the psychology of investors: how they make decisions and why.

- No matter where you get your funding, you must keep your investors up-to-date and informed. Communication is key. As you become engrossed in your business, you will tend to trade the time this takes against an operating issue or opportunity in the business. You must find time to communicate.

- Investors want consistency and professional communication. They do not want surprises—particularly negative ones. Consistency builds confidence and trust and establishes greater credibility.
- If you decide to raise money from friends and family and/or angels, try to limit the number of investors involved. Drafting paperwork and seeking signatures during later stages of funding is time consuming and expensive. Try to set a minimum investment amount you are willing to accept from each investor (for example, $50,000).
- Perform your own due diligence on potential investors. And, most important, don't be afraid to turn down a potential investor if you sense the wrong fit.

Focus, Feedback, and Flexibility

JILL BE NIMBLE, JILL BE QUICK

You may have to fight a battle more than once to win it.

Margaret Thatcher

Think of these three words—focus, feedback, and flexibility—as your mantra and a reminder that the only constant in business is change. *Focus* is the ability to intensely concentrate on a singular priority. *Feedback* is the reaction you will receive in response to your idea, your product, and your business and how it is perceived. And *flexibility* is your capacity to be limber and responsive to this feedback and to changes in your business. These are interrelated and necessary skills.

FOCUS

Focus is the ability that allows the entrepreneur to move from having that enormous passion, that great vision, to executing a strategy and creating a business.

When you're focused, you're constantly thinking about your idea, and in ways that others might not understand. You begin to see the whole world through the lens of your business idea. And once you're in that zone, a certain positive momentum is unleashed. Your mind runs with your idea and leads you to the next step, the next stage, and the next opportunity.

The need for focus is at the heart of running all businesses; for early-stage companies, it is absolutely essential. Focus helps you to weigh the numerous alternatives you will encounter in deciding the direction of your business and to discern where to spend your valuable time and energy. It is an overarching discipline that locks you on to that particular slice of the world that will become your domain. But be aware that the intense focus that drives you to success in one area can sometimes cause problems in others.

. . . .

The story of Health Payment Review (HPR) begins in 1988 when CEO Marcia Radosevich and her team built a clinical rule-based software system that helped manage the cost and quality of health care by ferreting out and foiling insurance fraud by doctors. It was designed to expose the bad apples who were overcharging insurers by breaking up medical procedures into their component parts and billing each one separately.

At the time, advisors told Marcia that the system she envisioned wouldn't be accepted because doctors would feel threatened and reject it out of hand. Marcia saw it differently. Although she respected such feedback, in her view the health care system was honest; her product would save insurers money, and in turn, that would save money for all in the patient-doctor-insurer chain. Marcia believed that only those doctors who abused the health insurance system would get caught. Legitimate doctors, on the other hand, helped her develop her product because they didn't like the "black eye" their profession was getting from dishonest colleagues.

Marcia's intense focus drove her forward—like a thoroughbred racehorse wearing blinders, she kept powering ahead. The potential customers she pursued were giants and included managed-care plans, insurance companies, HMOs, and large corporations that were self-insured. But Marcia's singular focus on this one product proved to be a double-edged sword:

> Once we actually got on our feet and launched our first product, it was a wild success and we were the darlings of the health care industry. Our product was selling like hotcakes and we were growing the company around it. My board of directors was looking ahead and asking me to come up with our next product. But I was so focused on our existing product that I kept saying, "Yeah, yeah, I'll think about that later."
>
> When you're starting a company and you're growing so rapidly, it's very, very hard to keep that dual focus between immediate needs and those indistinct and often invisible needs of the future. The net of it was that I was so busy growing the company that I kept meaning to put together a new product team and think about what our next new product would be. I just didn't get around to doing it.

Marcia had received appropriate feedback from her board, but given how fast her product was growing, she chose to ignore it at the time. That is, until a major competitor for Marcia's *only* product showed up on the scene. For the first time, Health Payment Review had to fight to remain dominant. Price erosion started to occur. "We needed a second act, but we didn't have one. We started to lose steam in the market. Morale dropped. As a group, we lacked vision for the future beyond our first product, and the result was that I lost some good people because they thought the company was a one-trick pony. We just weren't prepared to get our second act together."

DIGGING DEEPER

Advisory Boards

Throughout this book we stress the importance of having a strong board of advisors. They can help you navigate the terrain and provide insights and guidance when at a crossroads.

Why Do I Need an Advisory Board?
- To bring knowledge of your industry space
- To bring knowledge of the best practices in your own and other industries
- To help you with strategic issues
- To work with you in setting and achieving milestones
- To provide contacts to potential customers, investors, suppliers, employees
- To lend instant credibility to your enterprise
- To work for you more as a personal advisor, as opposed to advising the company "at large"
- To offer functional expertise (i.e., technology, marketing, financial)
- To provide the "been there, done that" lessons

How Do I Develop an Advisory Board?
- Identify ideal qualities and experience sought (e.g., industry experiences, functional expertise, start-up experience, raising capital) and strive to attain a mix of perspectives
- Use your network to find candidates
- Attend industry conferences and search for experts

(continues)

- Document guidelines and set expectations for participation on both sides
- Always be prepared when meeting; do not waste their time
- Formalize relationship with a job description and contract laying out expectations and deliverables (see Tool Kit on page 218 for a sample advisory board engagement)

What Qualities Should I Look for in Advisory Board Members?
- Integrity
- Consistency of values
- Reputation
- Successful track record
- Availability and accessibility; go for someone who will work for you, not someone who is a "name brand" and won't get involved in the heavy lifting
- Chemistry
- Willingness to challenge you; not a rubber stamp

How Does an Advisory Board Differ from the Board of Directors?
- It is an informal group of people
- Commonly used by early-stage companies prior to creating a formal board
- An advisory board is created to benefit the CEO and geared to your company's growth, not corporate governance
- A formal board of directors may be a statutory requirement; seek legal advice regarding what size board is necessary
- A board of directors has fiduciary responsibility and legal obligations to the shareholders of the company, not to the CEO

Then, during this very bleak time, a small miracle occurred in the form of an excellent niche company in their industry that was looking to be acquired. As a buying frenzy ensued, executives of this company who knew Marcia and one of her advisors well suggested that HPR buy them out, instead of the competition; this was just what they needed to kick-start a renewed phase of growth. HPR successfully took over the product, breathing new life into it. This new product, in turn, became the second act that saved the company. And, as they say, the rest is history.

Marcia took quick action to ensure that her company would have staying power. "From that moment on, I created a committee of new product development people and I chaired the group myself." She put structure and process into place and religiously rolled out a new product every ten months. Her management principles, her first-class ideas, and her ability to focus, take in feedback, and adapt to change proved out. Her company skyrocketed again and was eventually acquired by a dominant company in the health care field for a sizeable price.

As Marcia's story illustrates, sometimes intense focus can lead you in the wrong direction. Those blinders that keep you pointed forward and charging ahead can be the very same ones that lead to tunnel vision, blocking potential threats as well as opportunities. At the same time that you're figuring out which balls to keep in the air, you have to keep an eye on the horizon and an ear to the ground. It's an awkward contortion, to say the least—and a hint of things to come. Flexibility, which Marcia was able to call upon to move forward, is critical, as you will see.

So when we speak of focus, we're not suggesting that you direct your attention exclusively to just one aspect of your business. No growing enterprise we know of has the luxury of working on only one thing at a time. As your business grows, your attention and energy need to be concentrated on the company's most pressing needs, both short and long term.

Focusing on the wrong thing is definitely a killer, no two ways about it. For one failed start-up, it was such a Trojan horse that led the company in the wrong direction and then caused its demise. Vistify was born in 1999 in the early days of Internet shopping. The company's plan was straightforward: to manufacture a kitchen countertop appliance called "the ibot," an electronic valet of sorts that would allow the consumer to order groceries, take-out food, and other "convenience" items. The ibot connected to the Internet and the consumer simply touched colored buttons on the screen without having to use a computer. This seemed like a bright idea whose time had come.

However, management fell in love with the ibot gizmo itself rather than the behind-the-scenes connectivity and "retailer buy-in" that was necessary. They designed a snazzy-looking device reminiscent of the Jetson's TV set. It was like building a car before you had built roads and gas stations. By the time they figured out what they really needed to focus on, they were out of both time and capital. The moral of the story: Focus on the right thing.

FEEDBACK

The ibots of the world are why feedback is so vital. It's kind of like listening to the traffic report on the radio as you drive to work. It's information that helps you to choose, alter, or stay your course. But unlike a radio report, feedback comes in many forms and from many sources, and is often subjective. Sometimes you ask for feedback from clients, employees, investors, advisors, or the guy standing behind you in line at Starbucks. And like it or not, sometimes these same people volunteer their opinions unasked. And, of course, sometimes feedback comes directly from the marketplace.

Patricia Pomerleau is a case in point. Her company, CEO Express, went from a small idea to a product to a business—almost overnight, and all because of rousing feedback from potential customers who told Patricia that they wanted her product and service. "When people ask me to tell them about my product, I say, 'It's time.' We give time back to people by doing the work of rounding up the parts of the Web they want and need."

Technically, CEO Express aggregates, filters, and edits diverse information from the Net in a customized way for executives via a software platform that customers can edit to suit their preferences and needs. Basically, it's an organized portal that deals with the executive as a total person, not just a businessperson.

Here's how things got started: CEO Express was born in 1996, when Patricia decided to make it easier for her and her friends to get around the Internet quickly by building a portal—a Web site that links to other Web sites. Then a senior executive in the hospital industry, she understood the way executives thought and their typical squeamishness about tinkering with this new technology called the Web. She plunked down $35 to register a domain name for CEO Express and launched a site "just for the fun of it."

A month later, when Patricia agreed to speak at a conference on the topic "What Every CEO Needs to Know About the Internet," she was told to expect an audience of between fifty and one hundred people. To everyone's surprise, four hundred people showed up. Later that day, she put her presentation online so that all those who couldn't squeeze into the meeting room could tap in. The volume of activity was so great that it crashed the high-speed Internet connection for the rest of the conference. Overwhelmed by this tremendous interest, Patricia's first thought was, "Oh, my God. This could be a business." Four weeks after that conference, 25,000 people were using the product and CEO Express was on its way. Now that's what we call feedback! Patricia didn't stop there. Even though her feedback was the best kind that an entrepreneur can imagine, she is moving forward to keep the momentum going by creating offshoots of her product for lawyers, accountants, and other professionals.

The feedback that Patricia got was a standing ovation. Clearly, that does not always happen. Feedback comes in many unexpected forms and often at inconvenient times. It can seem overwhelmingly positive or amazingly negative. For sound decisionmaking, it is important to sort it all out and weigh the information with a judicious and balanced eye.

Sometimes feedback is so negative and comes from such an authoritative source that the best thing you can do is take it, cut your losses, and go back to the drawing board. But most often, feedback is based on some combination of fact and opinion. It is always colored by the personal experiences and projections of the person providing it, so it's up to you to net it out and, in the process, discover a way of overcoming it. Consider the source of the feedback—who is giving it and why; then evaluate it accordingly. Most of all, listen to your gut and trust your instincts. Ask yourself whether this person is objective. Go back and make sure that your market is there. Ask whether this person's motivations are well intentioned. Are their interests aligned with yours or frankly to the contrary? We call this skill of picking the wheat from the chaff "navigating the naysayers."

· · · ·

Paula White of 600 lb gorillas is a navigator to rival Magellan. As she noted, "*Everybody* is an expert, so *who* do you listen to?" Since starting her company with her husband, Chris, in 1999, Paula has developed skin as thick as that of a rhinoceros from hearing constantly negative feedback, and a sixth sense for processing it. In the beginning, she heard "You'll never be able to do it" so many times that it was one of the reasons behind the company name: "*600 lb gorillas.*" And it came as no surprise to Paula that most people she talked to hated the name.

The product that inspires so much instant expertise is in fact a simple one: premium, all-natural frozen cookie dough balls. Pop a few dough balls from the freezer into the oven and you have fresh "homemade" cookies. Although this sounds easy enough, successful execution from the business perspective is anything but.

In the food industry, shelf space is the name of the game. Period. For a little upstart company, no matter how innovative the product, competing with Pillsbury and the other behemoths is akin to David facing Goliath. Add the virtual lack of an advertising budget and the odds look even less appealing.

Yet the company has been successful, and Paula attributes this to several factors: eschewing conventional wisdom, skillfully processing negative feedback, building an advisory board, and working her network.

Early on, after *everyone* had told her that she'd never get her cookies into a supermarket, *finally* someone suggested that the way to get her cookies into a store is through distributors. These guys are the established channel for the grocery industry. Problem: Not one distributor would talk to her. So, armed with insights from an advisor, Paula muscled her way directly to supermarket buyers: "I thought that if the distributor wouldn't listen, then maybe the store buyers would. But I knew I'd have to have some proof. And I knew that it would take customers to get their attention. I went to a food show, had people sample the cookies, and asked them to fill out a simple survey card saying they would buy 600 lb gorillas if their local supermarket carried them. I collected over five hundred cards, and then I set out to identify the 'right' decision-maker at the chains, the ones looking for a differentiating edge, and set my sights on reaching them." She got her audience, and they loved her product. And getting attention didn't stop there.

The last time we saw Paula, she was decked out in her safari outfit, pith helmet and all. Along with Chris, who was wearing the wooly gorilla suit, she was setting up shop in a mock bamboo hut in Costco, the giant wholesale club. And how did she get into this highly desirable retailer? The name that everyone hated—the 600 lb gorilla—which Paula chose in part to make up for the lack of an advertising budget—opened the door. And as we write this, Paula's product is in seven hundred stores in New England, representing 100 percent penetration of the major chains in this territory; and, by the way, her test with Costco went amazingly well.

Sometimes I feel like the "Little Engine That Could." I've had so much negative feedback that I've developed my own system for processing it. First, I evaluate the person and their criteria to assess whether they have relevant experience qualifying them to "critique" in the first place. I was not afraid to ask directly what was driving their commentary; this is especially critical.

Next, I'd put any feedback to the test in the field. Customers always have the "final say." Sometimes, I just take my packag-

ing out to a grocery store and test it on the floor with customers. It doesn't take a lot of money. Then finally there comes
a point when you just have to block out the pessimists, ignore
the draining negative energy, and trust your own instincts. Because I've learned so much over these last three years, I can just
go with my gut.

. . . .

Whether from a trusted mentor or another source, the greatest
failing of an entrepreneur regarding feedback is to become defensive. It is your baby they're talking about. It is your dream,
your sweat and tears. You have lived day and night nurturing
your idea into reality. And now some cruel outsider comes
along and stomps all over your fledgling enterprise with their
hobnailed boots. Naturally your instinct is to declare them
wrong ("But you just don't understand!") and reject what
they have to say. It is precisely when you are experiencing
such feelings that you need to stop, take a deep breath (sigh if
you must), and listen. Listen to comprehend what is really
being said and to understand answers, not to explain or defend. And remember, once you have truly and objectively understood what has been said, you are always free to reject it.
When you have processed it completely, do what Paula did:
Take action.

Although critical feedback can be difficult to hear, the information it imparts can be more valuable than positive input. As
one of our entrepreneur friends puts it, "Feedback is the breakfast of champions." Unless the feedback comes in the form of
the bank padlocking your office door, feedback is yours to consider, and then to accept or reject.

FLEXIBILITY

Flexibility is the ability to adapt to change by absorbing new information, processing it through your focus filter, and making the appropriate adjustments so that your business survives and prospers.

Meet Antoinette Bruno, CEO of Star Chefs, which is an online culinary magazine coupled with a classified online job board for the food industry. With traffic exceeding over 12.5 million hits a month, it's become an entrenched source for those in the industry. We have all come to know Antoinette and we think of her as the poster girl for flexibility.

During the last few years, Antoinette has had to reinvent, redesign and reconfigure her business several times due to changes in virtually everything around her. First came the bursting of the Internet bubble; this was when she "morphed" her business plan from "B2C" to "B2B" (Internet-speak for "business to consumer" and "business to business" models). Then came the weakened economy, and along with that endless advice from every direction—her customers, her partners, her investors.

Star Chefs' corporate headquarters is in New York City's famous Flat Iron district, the jumping-off point for many leading-edge restaurants and their innovative chefs. Wearing a vintage Courrèges suit and Manolo Blahnik shoes, Antoinette remembered back to the summer of 1999 when the Star Chefs founders hired her. Her charge: Take the company to the next level. She was given a business plan and told to execute it. Although Antoinette and her partner thought then that an online magazine with a traditional advertising model and classified ad section was the way to go, she wasn't given much choice. "Pursue the uncharted waters of e-commerce" was her mandate:

About this time the Internet was cresting. We were offered funding for two different business models, one from private investors for the classifieds plan, the other from one of the largest manufacturers of food service equipment, for a modified e-commerce plan. The founders said "No way!" to the classified plan I clearly favored because the dollars from the equipment manufacturer were so much bigger. So, this time, we bit. We signed a letter of agreement with the manufacturer and I was so happy that I left for a long-overdue and needed vacation. My timing could not have been worse. About a week later, the stock market crashed and I knew in my gut that the manufacturer would back out of our deal.

I said to my partner, "We're never going to get this money. I know it." Given the turn in the environment, it was inevitable. The forces were just too great and it was only a matter of time before the equipment manufacturer was gone.

Fortunately, I quickly stopped all plans to build their e-commerce platform. This, I am sure, is the reason we're still in business today. We had gone from one full-time employee and a few part-timers to twenty-five people on the strength of those projections. Then I had to cut the staff in half. I did it over a two-month period because I didn't want to put the whole system into shock. Then I slowly peeled back, and we were down to seven people a year later.

It happened again to Antoinette after she ignited the audience at a major food industry convention. Companies of incredible stature approached her to help them design online training programs for their entry-level employees. In turn, they promised development dollars to bring the project forward. She took some time to seek out video game producers to help her with this project, but then realized that, as tantalizing as this could have been, it was not a guarantee. She ultimately passed when she saw it would take too much time and capital, both financial and human, to develop even a pilot without a signed contract in hand.

We applaud Antoinette for her flexibility in navigating these twists and turns, all the while keeping her company moving ahead; but a lot of major—and, in retrospect, unnecessary—detours arose because of reacting to feedback from potential investors. We call this the "following-the-money syndrome," and it's something all CEOs who are raising capital need to watch out for. How far do you go to attract a potential investor? In your sometimes desperate quest for funding, you can easily veer off course from your original vision. For Star Chefs, many different business models were tried; from the perspective of perfect "20/20 hindsight," they may have gone in too many different directions—by Antoinette's reckoning, as many as eight different business models. As she told us, "We've gone full circle and are back to where we first started." It's a dizzying story.

A turning point for Antoinette was her meeting of mentors, those she had come to trust in a short time. After auditioning in Boston for a coveted slot to present at an upcoming venture capital forum called Springboard, where "chosen" entrepreneurs present their companies and plans to prospective investors, she had the opportunity to "pitch" again before an informal gathering of angel investors, who took Antoinette under their wings. They weren't wowed by her industry or business model, but rather by her knowledge of her market and the opportunity, and, most of all, by how well she sought, listened, and responded to feedback.

Because going from business model to business model and from market to market had been an overwhelming experience for Antoinette, she found the group's interest in her nourishing and fortifying. Their specific advice: Focus on where the pain existed in her industry. This was all she needed to hear. It validated what she had been thinking all along. "Finding and hiring new employees is a major issue for the restaurant industry. Employing over 17 million people annually, with an employee turnover rate of 120 percent, means that the average worker doesn't even stay on the job for a full year. That's pain. We were already in the business of labor with the Job Finder. We just weren't focusing on it."

Star Chefs is now back to its roots and a combination of "all the good of the past." It is a popular site for those in the restaurant trade and the food aficionados Antoinette calls "foodies." Revenues are generated from advertising and from classified ad fees from the Job Finder, the company's proprietary technology platform. This online job board has a niche focus and today is the most specialized site on the Web for anyone looking for work in the food industry—from wait staff to executive chefs. It's a virtual employment marketplace and it's working.

DIGGING DEEPER

More on Mentors

The importance of a mentor in your life is critical. As you are bombarded with feedback from all directions, it helps to have a trusted person looking out for your best interests. A good deal has been written about mentors and the vital role they play in an entrepreneur's development. And for good reason. Mentors are wise and loyal guides, advisors, or teachers who help entrepreneurs grow, and—just as important—develop. Good mentors share core traits. They are nonjudgmental, empathetic, affirming, and always candid, even when the news may not be what you want to hear.

Mentors can be any age and gender, and are found in any number of places. For instance, they can be long-time confidants, former

(continues)

teachers, early bosses, or industry gurus. There are a growing number of business organizations and professionals that provide mentoring, or have formal groups trained to provide this support.

Getting the Most from Your Mentor

- Make sure that important building blocks are in place. Agree on expectations and make sure your commitments to the relationship are mutual. Don't expect your mentor to be more committed to your growth than you are.
- Value this relationship and treat it with respect. Establish a time frame for your engagement and agree on a process for your working relationship. Schedule periodic reviews.
- Enter the relationship in a trusting frame of mind and commit to being truthful at all times. Make sure your working chemistry is compatible; this is a must.
- Respect the role of your mentor and do not overimpose or act inappropriately. Remember, your mentor is not a therapist, a parent, or a banker; rather, he or she is a coach, a listener, and a connector.

And so the cycle rolls—focus, feedback and flexibility—like the figure eight, the loop keeps going. That virtuous cycle of focus, feedback, and flexibility never ends. Even after reaching ambitious milestones, inevitably there will be other goals, new challenges, and another set of targets waiting around the bend. If you focus on what's in front of you, you'll find that positive momentum will build. And, if you're like the entrepreneurs we know, you'll seek qualified feedback. You'll listen, sort the wheat from the chaff, adapt by flexibly tweaking your idea and—you'll move forward, again.

Our next chapter is about just that; moving forward from the hand-to-mouth existence of starting your business to a more stable growing stage and new level of leadership. You'll learn firsthand how leadership styles can influence the growth and culture of your enterprise.

WHAT YOU NEED TO KNOW

- It is a guarantee that your business plan will change over time.
- Focus implies intensity, but not rigidity. Do not become overly wedded to your original assumptions.
- Be prepared when investors weigh in and want you to dilute your focus by asking you to evaluate new products or markets for your company. Assess carefully whether the shift in focus will pay off in a greater future for the company.
- Sometimes an entrepreneur can be so focused that she creates a dysfunctional distance between her team and herself. Make sure others in your company receive communication and feedback that reflects your current thinking.
- Remember that all feedback, whether positive or negative, contains valuable information. It may not be information that you should act upon.
- Understand the motivation and psychology of those who give you feedback.
- Particularly in investors' meetings, you may be tested by someone playing the role of devil's advocate. Be prepared for this and respond in a calm and thoughtful manner. The investor may be testing how you respond under pressure.
- Whether you agree or disagree, always listen to feedback and thank those giving it. Starting to argue or push back will make you look defensive.

- There is a difference between flexibility in responding to a significant change in the environment and getting pulled off track by distractions that are not essential to your business. Be alert to such differences.
- You can be flexible and adaptive while still remaining true to your original vision.
- It is imperative to find mentors and advisors who can help you shift through feedback and respond accordingly.
- Above all, when receiving feedback, look out for the signals telling you that are becoming defensive. If they are there, take a deep breath, bury the "Yeah, but," and listen to understand.

CHAPTER 8

Leadership Lessons

PEOPLE BUILD COMPANIES

*Leadership should be born out of the understanding
of the needs of those who would be affected by it.*

Marian Anderson

Whether you're a born leader or learning to lead as you hit the ground running, three of your most immediate responsibilities as the head of a new company are to set the culture, communicate and gain commitment to your vision, and hire the people who can make this vision a reality.

. . . .

"Culture" is the often-used term to describe the soul of your company. It's a reflection of your values and your personality, and it's embodied in the principles, operating procedures, and processes of your company. If a company were a person, its culture would be its values, personality, and behavior. Everything follows from your company's culture because it is the foundation upon which you build your business. It informs the critical decisions you make and the actions you take, as well as those you choose to pass over.

133

And be mindful: No matter what values you espouse, your behavior, not your words, will define your culture. Culture is about what you do and how you do it, not your words.

No two approaches are exactly the same; still, your leadership style should inspire and empower your staff to devote themselves to the manifestation of your vision—to make it their dream, too. Your consistent behavior and action as you lead the charge is essential for building trust among all your constituents—your employees, customers, vendors, and investors alike. The culture you instill in your organization will determine how your company holds together in good times—and in bad. It can make or break your company now and in the long term. It's that important.

Case in point: Tena Clark is the founder and CEO of Disc-Marketing. She has been in the music business all her life as a songwriter, composer, and producer of music for film and television. In 1998, Tena's belief in the power of music sparked her vision and led to the creation of a new marketing medium that combines music, multimedia, and Internet interaction into one product that entertains as it dispenses information about the client's product or service, called an "ECD," short for "enhanced CD ROM."

Here's an example of how Tena's company works: In 2002, mega-retailer Target came to DiscMarketing looking for a way to pump up toy sales for Christmas. DiscMarketing created an ECD for Target's customers to use with their home computers. The ECD was packed with games and music and, more to the point, displayed seventy-five toys that the kids and their parents could scrutinize and play with virtually. Then they could print a list of their favorite toys, or go online and purchase them directly from Target.

DiscMarketing's promotion for Target not only worked—it worked big. Tena has since created many bull's-eye successes for other retailers, as well as advertising agencies, large corporations, and even the government. She proudly smiles when she talks about her roster of delighted customers: "Our clients are the big guys: Coke, the U.S. Army, 7-Up, General Mills, Mead-Johnson. We are one of the fastest growing companies in America."

From her converted headquarters inside the oldest firehouse in Pasadena, California, Tena exudes the tremendous enthusiasm that has been the driving force behind her company for the five years of its existence. She credits much of DiscMarketing's success to its corporate culture. "There are more than sixty of us now. We're like a family and my people are so afraid we're going to lose that feeling as we get bigger, but I won't let it happen. I'll stop the growth before we become just another bureaucratic corporate entity. The trust my people have in my values is just as important to me as our success. Because that's where our success comes from."

Tena's philosophy is to match, as best she can, the talents of her staff to their jobs and then personally convey her belief in them. Such faith inspires their confidence and reinforces their commitment. Tena is sure that's the reason they give 150 percent—very important when the company is close to capacity and projects are stacking up in the queue.

There are people here on the weekend and at night because this company is about building a dream. And what I tell all my employees and staff so many times they're probably sick of hearing it is that, in the end, whether the business is sold or I retire, my biggest dream is that I can walk out this door knowing that every person in this company felt they started something from nothing, that they were part of a big vision, that they were able to fulfill their financial goals for their families, have the home they wanted, do the things they wanted to do, have a blast and, also, that they were cared about.

As a company, we are an amazing think tank. Every person's brain is respected here. I don't care what a person's title is. If they have an idea, I will always listen. And it has genuinely empowered people. Today, two of my multimedia guys e-mailed me and wanted to set up a lunch because they have an idea they want to run by me. I love that. Whether they're the runner or the head 3-D animator, they know they have access to me.

Tena's values also have an impact on her client roster. When she was in the music business she would never write a song with racy lyrics or anything that would embarrass her "in front of God or her children," as she explained it. "I try to do the same thing with this company. I will not work on cigarette products because my mom and dad both died of lung cancer. I guess what I'm trying to say is that I hope that my kids can say that what I did I did with integrity, and that I really made a positive difference in the lives of the people who work for me."

The hallmarks of Tena's leadership style are respect, teamwork, innovation, and responsibility. When you are in her presence and mesmerized by her charm, you realize that she has built her company on the strength of her charismatic personality. Often the power of an individual's personality is a major contributor to the company's personality. It can be a "lead the charge" enthusiasm or a quiet strength. Whichever way it manifests itself, the leader's vision and her values are such a part of who she is that they can't be separated from the personality of the organization—nor should they be. As you are entering the world of business or you find your company growing beyond your wildest dreams, be yourself and stay true to yourself. Don't think that you need to transform the essence of the person you truly are—which, in fact, may be your biggest selling point. Just keep the following in mind:

- The purpose of a company's culture is to serve the organization, not the other way around.
- Some aspects of culture are visible, others are not. You can see how people dress, how offices are laid out, and how customers, suppliers, and employees are treated. You cannot see what's invisible—values, intentions, and core beliefs about the best way to run a business.
- The kind of business you are in—the industry, geography, size, staff diversity, and the company's life stage—all will have influence in shaping your culture.
- Leaders are responsible for maintaining culture and should try to change it only when it is absolutely essential. Changing culture is like trying to change your personality.
- When challenge is afoot, or change is required, focus on your core values—the things that matter most—and use them to guide crucial decisions.

· · · ·

When Lori Shaefer, CEO of Marketmax, joined a company that was in desperate need of reinvention, she committed to this adopted dream as if it were her own. Since 1997, Lori has imbued Marketmax with a never-say-die culture that much reflects the kind of leader she is for her more than two hundred employees. The wall behind her desk is covered with pictures of herself and her family hiking up mountains, white-water rafting, running, and golfing; in the middle of it all is a dramatic lettered sign that reads, "Don't Quit." This motto is her touchstone and that of her company.

Marketmax is a software company whose product helps retailers manage their inventories, choose the products customers will want most, and set the right pricing, promotion, and shelf placement, all factors that improve profitability. Lori's client list ranges from leading-edge specialty retailers to department stores and huge Internet players such as Home Depot and Amazon.com, as well as the suppliers who sell to these establishments.

Lori's background is in mathematics and marketing, and she was hired away from Procter and Gamble by the founder of Marketmax, who brought her in to resuscitate the company. "At that time, it was a very, very small start-up. I essentially took over a company that was about to close down."

Lori "fell in love" with this company and went to extremes she would definitely not recommend to others: "I did crazy things strictly out of belief, will, and passion, because I wanted so much for the company to survive. The company was badly in debt, and because there were no investors who thought the company had a chance of survival, I bankrolled the company with my personal credit, used credit cards to pay the payroll and even the IRS. I took out a home equity loan and between that, the credit cards, and my personal savings, I went into the hole to the tune of $800,000." Doing that entailed great personal sacrifice for herself and her family, not something we recommend. Lori didn't necessarily think it was the wisest course to take, but as she succinctly put it, "It was do or die."

It took Lori three years to get out from under that debt, and it made her an extremely creative entrepreneur in every sense. She lived poorly until the company was in the black; meanwhile, Marketmax signed on reputable customers who believed in the product and paid on time. After all that, it felt easy to find venture capital money.

"What kept me going was that I really, really believed in the company. I knew my customers well. I had a few employees and they had families, and I was not about to let any of them down. I also believed in the tremendous potential of Marketmax because core customers—CEOs of major retail companies—assured me it was a valuable idea and that they needed us. If they believed in me when we were nothing but a vision, there had to be something to the concept." What fueled Lori was also her belief in herself. "I'm a driven person; we're going to do it."

The story of Marketmax is one of survival with a culture sprung from adversity; one shaped by too much debt, foregone salaries, overwhelming workloads. The people with whom Lori surrounded herself had the fortitude and willingness to sacrifice because they believed in Lori and in the company.

It was Lori's "Don't Quit" attitude that set the tone. Her example of personal sacrifice and willingness to "give it her all" were the motivational juices that nourished the rest of the team. She never expected anyone to do anything that she was not prepared to do herself. In return, the team would go to the mat for her. Although the early days were like an episode of *Survivor,* today Marketmax is solid, profitable, and achieving major customer wins in the highly competitive and cut-throat retail arena. You'll still find employees working late into the night or giving up weekends because they are pushing hard to win that next big retailer for their growing and impressive client roster. The culture that first shaped Marketmax is intact today because it continues to fit the company's business; and, more important, it still suits the leader of the business—and it's working.

A company often starts with a person and a dream and very little else. There's no product, no accounting system, no infrastructure, no technology, and no staff. As you put these necessary pieces in place by building safeguards to support the business, optimizing scarce resources, and establishing operating practices, processes, and procedures, more likely than not you'll learn that many of the skills critical to building the business are quite different from the talents you originally brought to the table.

One of the most important learned traits is delegating. Critical to executing your plan is to transfer substantive responsibilities as the company grows. You need to focus your time and energy in areas that will yield the highest return based on your innate talents. Although letting go is difficult, it is also a mark of leadership maturity. Nobody does everything well. Keep what you do well and delegate the rest.

Delegating can be challenging because from day one, when you were the first employee of the company, you had to micromanage every detail. Why? Because there was no one else to do it. The problem is that micromanaging becomes a habit that is hard to break even when you have hired perfectly competent people. The two greatest reasons an entrepreneur can't keep "her hands off the blocks" are a feeling of losing control and the belief that she can do it better than anyone else can.

One of your most critical responsibilities as a leader will be recruiting top talent. And top talent doesn't usually enjoy taking orders from someone else and doing unchallenging work. To attract and keep great people, you will have to entrust them with the responsibility—as well as the authority—to do the job. You must believe in them, support them, and then stand back and let them rise (and sometimes fall) to the occasion. You will likely need to resist the urge to go back to ruling the entire roost and learn instead to delegate the responsibilities that others can handle as well as and, as shocking as it may sound, maybe better than you.

Keep in contact with all layers of the company and meet regularly with those you designate as your core management team. Delegating does not mean abdicating. You have to be able to ferret out who is doing a great job and who is more style than substance; who is getting a great return on her efforts and who is always asking for more resources. Some CEOs we know have an open-space office plan and place themselves right in the thick of the action. This helps them monitor the company's pulse directly. Not a prerequisite by any means, but not a bad idea in the early days.

A pioneer from the early days of the technology revolution, Lore Harp McGovern is now a private investor. She was the founder and CEO of the highly successful Vector Graphics, a computer hardware manufacturer that she started long before people used the term "personal computer." Lore was also masterful at connecting with people. "I would walk around every Monday and spend time on the manufacturing floor. I'd stop and talk to people so that they really felt connected to what was going on. Regularly I would give a 'state of the company' message, always on the manufacturing floor where everybody came together and we just talked about what was happening."

Initially, Lore knew everybody by name:

I had an association with each employee. I knew their personal stories, knew when somebody had a baby, knew when somebody got married. As we grew, I realized that I didn't know everybody any longer, so I instituted "Lunch with Lore" and once a month I would invite ten people. Any employee could sign up and we would go out to a good restaurant and I would learn about what they were thinking, what they were doing, and how they viewed happenings within the company. These lunches were always full and I could sense that employees were interested in maintaining two-way communications. I heard about the great things going on, but people also felt free to share problems and other thorny issues.

As well as keeping in touch with the people who work for you, you have to keep an eye and ear on the world outside your company's walls. Part of your leadership task is to interpret the external environment and how it impacts your company. You continuously have to build relationships with customers and monitor competitors. If you become too insular, you can miss bulletins from the marketplace that you need to know about to adjust your strategy. Achieving a balance between ground-floor engagement and top-floor management with a window into the rest of the world takes practice, but it's what you're aiming for.

Lore McGovern's leadership style was inclusive. People felt connected to her and, as a result, the company they worked for. This may sound simple; however, it is often the simplest constructs that are the hardest to execute. Empowerment that derives from feeling part of an organization inspires people to greatness and to go that extra mile because they will share in the company's success. Imbuing a company with the belief that everyone's contributions will have an impact on the direction and well-being of the company is one of the most important roles you have as a leader. Recognizing and acknowledging these contributors visibly and rewarding them accordingly is a "must do."

This "managing by walking around" is important. It gives you visibility, lets people know you care, and offers the opportunity to compliment someone who is doing something well. It also gives you a vital information link to the people who really know what's going on. One caveat: The spirit of such exposure is for you to support and listen. If it ever takes on the character of undermining your managers, checking up on them, or looking for defects and shortfalls, the culture will quickly turn into one of fear and resentment, of lacking honesty, and of doing what is politically expedient.

One of the most difficult things, but the most rewarding, is to hire the best people you possibly can. Marcia Radosevich of Health Payment Review, whose story we recounted in Chapter 7, knows full well the challenges faced in managing a high-growth company. Marcia is highly individualistic and expects others to be that way, too. So when she began recruiting her team, she viewed it as an opportunity to bring in the best people for the job, Ph.D.s and M.D.s, people who often are not a recruiter's top choice in a traditional corporate structure. And once she had these high-potential performers in the company, she understood that an important aspect of her growth and that of her company was to make sure not only that she didn't micromanage them but that she empowered them to enhance and execute on the company's plan.

> I purposely sought out people who were brighter than I was, who were better at their jobs than I could have been. And I told them, 'If you can't do your job better than I can, then I've hired the wrong person.' I didn't need to be the loudest voice in the room. I didn't want to be the dictator. I can make the tough decisions and I will make them when I have to, but I prefer decisions to be more cooperative. I think that that leads to a better decision. I

also think it means that people really buy into it so then they're going to kill themselves to prove themselves right as opposed to proving me right. When you're growing a company, finding the right people is the most important thing a CEO can do. And it's also one of the things that CEOs often tend to put off because it's so time consuming and the reward is out there in the future.

Marcia created a supportive environment for her highly skilled staff. Then she got out of the way and let them work. Her management style paid off handsomely. By giving her people a great deal of autonomy and authority, they were invested emotionally and economically in the success of the venture.

Groups of people build companies—it's not just one whirling dervish trying to do it all. To build a really world-class business you have to be introspective enough to understand your weak points, see where you need to add other people to bolster these areas, hire these people, and let them go. Focus your attention on key strategic areas. Forget about trying to perform the many tasks that you used to.

Clearly, one of the key groups that you need to enroll in your vision will be your future employees. Because start-ups, by definition, are risky, and because you won't have a lot of money for payroll, people won't be coming to work for either financial or job security. But they will come to your fresh new company if you're able to articulate your vision so that they're excited about getting in on the ground floor and participating in the challenges of breaking new ground.

We have all heard the refrain, "people are our most important asset." Unfortunately, to some executives, that's all they are. We encourage you to view your employees as critical to your ultimate success. Set up processes to interview selected candidates professionally and carefully. Probe into their past experience and look for patterns of behavior. Bill Byham, CEO of DDI, Inc., a highly successful human resource consulting firm, insists that hiring "isn't just a matter of luck," and that it can be as disciplined as any other business decision.

For Tena Clark of DiscMarketing, her biggest hiring challenge hasn't been attracting people; rather, it's been hiring people who have the potential to keep up with the explosive growth of her company:

> When I started, I always wanted to hire the best people, but there was no way I could afford them. So I'd make hiring decisions I *could* afford, and in two months we outgrew those people and I had to go out and hire again.
>
> I used to fly around the country, 150,000 miles a year, because I was a one-person show when it came to closing really big deals. I finally realized that I had to find other people who could do the job for us to realize our full potential. When you get the size we are and are still growing, you can't all stand in a circle and sing "Kumbaya" every day. Sometimes you have to make tough decisions.
>
> I've also had to let go people whom I absolutely adored, but the team was suffering because they were not functioning at a higher level of expertise. When our sales people, our creative people, and our client services department are working with senior people from Coke and Target and the top talent at ad agencies every day, your team has to be at that same level. There are ten people in the company who've been with me from the beginning and I'm lucky that I have them. And now I finally have my dream team.

If you're feeling a little overwhelmed by the unrelenting nature of leadership, we want to assure you that women unequivocally make great leaders. Many attributes required of leaders today are innate in women. They may simply need to be developed and applied to business. We know firsthand that women are collaborative, and are quick studies. We find they are empathetic, can nurture when needed, and easily relate to others. They form partnerships and build teams and communities extremely well. They see multiple points of view and seek inclusivity. They can multitask as easily as they can singularly focus. They are highly intuitive and use their intuition when facts and data for a particular decision are sparse. They are also adept at self-assessment and are able to seek advice when they need it.

DIGGING DEEPER

Why Women Make Great Leaders
We are "hard-wired" with skills to be great leaders:

- Multitasking—we know how to keep many balls in the air
- Empathy—innate ability to forge connections, seek multiple points of view, inclusivity
- Realistic self-assessment—recognizing and understanding gaps in our skill set, seeking help and advice when there is no home-grown expertise
- Natural resource optimizers
- Natural collaborators and partnership builders

It is important to point out behaviors in the business world that often are associated with women. Here is a list of actions to guard against; they can negatively impact your effectiveness as well as the perception of your effectiveness:

(*continues*)

- Thinking too small
- Being too conservative
- Taking "it" personally
- Fearing to make a mistake
- Second-guessing yourself
- Not tooting your own horn
- Stylistically not seeming confident
- Wanting people to like you
- Hedging
- Abdicating final decisionmaking

Metamorphosing from the very early stage—for some, a survival stage—through to a more stable growth phase is the first major transition period a company faces. In the next chapter, we talk to entrepreneurs who've gone beyond the base-building years of their business, and we'll shine a light on the ongoing challenges one can expect. They have much to say about managing a company out into the future.

WHAT YOU NEED TO KNOW

- Culture is the manifestation of the values you live by. It will be the cornerstone of your success. Competitors can copy your products, services, and pricing, but they can't "me-too" a high-performance, exciting, and fulfilling culture. Your culture is distinctive, as well it should be.
- Be prepared to encourage, solicit, and listen to employee and customer feedback. Once you have it, thank

them for it, make relevant decisions, and let them know whether or not you used their ideas and why.

- Vision is the brass ring; but day-to-day execution gets you there. A vision alone is not enough; it must have an underlying strategy and plan that is the path you will follow.
- Remember that as you grow, you will continue to face challenges and setbacks. As always, make the best decisions you can at the time and move on. Don't dwell on your mistakes; learn from them.
- People build companies. Consciously, make the effort to recognize and acknowledge the contribution of your team and all its members and give them specific positive feedback. Look for opportunities to catch someone doing something properly.
- Being a leader and being a manager are two very different things. A leader creates an environment in which people inspire and motivate themselves. A manager is more involved in the day-to-day operations of the company. As an entrepreneur, you must wear both hats.
- Play the hand you're dealt. You can't always control what happens to you, but you can control how you respond to it. This way of thinking gave rise to the saying, "If life gives you lemons, make lemonade."
- Don't be afraid to assert yourself. Although no one wants a domineering, micromanaging "boss," too often entrepreneurs are willing to subjugate their personalities and natural strengths in favor of inclusion, consensus, or not hurting peoples' feelings. Be who you are, be open to feedback and personal change, and run the ship.

- Tell the truth. Foster a culture of truth telling. This starts with you. Honestly share the bad news with the good. Let people know the strategy of the company and your current thinking; encourage others to do the same. Talk candidly to people about their performance issues. Above all, when bad news comes to you, don't shoot the messenger.

CHAPTER 9

Life After the Survival Stage

MANAGING ONWARD

Life loves to be taken by the lapel and told, "I'm with you, kid. Let's go."

Maya Angelou

Congratulations! Your business is alive and kicking and your company is squarely in the game. You're moving from the infancy stage to the growth stage, a period that comes with a decidedly different set of challenges and obstacles, as well as promising possibilities that you couldn't have imagined even a year earlier.

Because of the maniacal focus in the early days of a business, it's common for entrepreneurs to find they haven't given much thought beyond surviving to the next day. Now the day is here. Savor the moment. You've earned it. However, just when you think you're out of the woods, you discover you're about to enter a whole new forest.

Now it's time to implement formal systems, controls, and processes; to make sure you've slotted the right people into the right jobs; to delegate key pieces of the action; and, if necessary, to reposition or replace employees who are incapable of meeting the company's future challenges.

Laying this foundation won't feel as adrenaline-charged as the high-octane days when you were bootstrapping and pitching your dream to strangers with pockets full of money. But building your company's infrastructure is just as important now as pioneering was before. In fact, this transition demands a higher level of competence, broadened strategic thinking, and sharpened decisionmaking skills.

Rhona Silver is a caterer extraordinaire, owner and operator of Long Island's Huntington Townhouse, an awe-inspiring 148,000-square-foot property complete with fifteen ballrooms, nine kitchens, and the capacity to cater everything from a corporate meeting to a mega–trade show.

But it wasn't always so.

When we met Rhona, she was elegantly attired in a fur-trimmed suit and working along with the serving staff setting up the buffet and the tapestry-and-lace-draped tables beneath magnificent chandeliers. She told how her business went through a survival stage that we know might have crushed a lesser spirit, and a growth phase in which she struggled to build another, even grander business on top of the first. "I'm inexpressibly happy," says Rhona. "My life is amazing, considering where I was and where I am now."

Rhona grew up in a catering family and from the age of ten knew she wanted to be in the business. When she got married, she forgot about her dream for a while. One night while attending a bar mitzvah with her Orthodox Jewish husband, Rhona had an epiphany: Kosher food was prepared and served in a lackluster way—she knew that people would appreciate excellent cuisine and elegant presentation.

Rhona recognized a need in the market, and by envisioning how she could channel her gift "for taking two morsels of food and creating a work of art," she hatched an idea for a premiere kosher catering business. Despite her husband's objections and the eventual dissolution of her marriage, Rhona was soon catering every kosher event on Long Island.

As the business prospered and grew beyond the capacity of her own kitchen, Rhona zeroed in on an unlikely site for a permanent headquarters. The Huntington Townhouse housed a failing catering business on a twenty-acre parcel adjacent to a burned-out shopping mall that developers had estimated would take from five to seven years to rebuild.

It was a site only a dreamer could love. Still, Rhona hurled her vision toward this daunting reality. "The truth is, I didn't know how to undertake due diligence, but my gut told me to buy this place. I had catered to the best: the Plaza, the Pierre, the Waldorf. I'd revolutionized the kosher catering industry by taking the standard from chicken on a plain white plate to works of art on magnificent china. I knew that if I could cater to one segment of the population and build an incredible business, I could cater to the whole world with the Townhouse. It needed a ton of work, but I had no doubt that I would eventually succeed."

And so began the growth phase of Rhona's business.

Thirty days after Rhona bought her dream site, the adjacent mall was sold to a businessman who had a vision as grand as hers. Soon, the mall alongside Rhona's twenty acres was occupied by Bloomingdale's, Lord & Taylor, and Saks Fifth Avenue, decidedly upscale entrants that made the Huntington Townhouse even more valuable by association.

It seemed that the success of her new venture was blessed and that her lucky stars were aligned. That is, until Rhona collided head-on with powerful moneyed institutions intent on under-mining her for their own gain. All entrepreneurs lie awake at night during the growth phase worrying about what can go wrong, and Rhona was no exception. But even her darkest nightmares couldn't prepare her for what was to come. "I'm very goal-oriented and focused, but the path was paved with broken glass."

To raise capital for her venture, Rhona leased her twenty acres to a management company for several million dollars a year, an agreement the lessor had no intention of honoring. Instead, he planned to force Rhona out of business, buy her property for a song, combine the acreage with that of the mall, and build apartment buildings and more retail footage on the site.

It was then that Rhona's mortgage banker notified her that the Townhouse mortgage was in default. "I couldn't under-stand how that could be true. Despite all that was going on, my payments were never a day late. I had refinanced my home to stay current on my payments because perfect credit was very important to me."

Rhona soon learned that the bank was in cahoots with the management company and had in fact violated the law by conjuring up a "technical default" to squeeze Rhona out of her now-prime location. Rhona hired excellent legal counsel, sued both parties, and ultimately prevailed. In spite of all this, Rhona's business quintupled. To put out elegant meals on a grand scale, she had brought on an exceptional staff: a hands-on chief financial officer (CFO), a core management team, and a highly skilled restaurant crew, including a world-class chef. They served her well during this potentially devastating time.

Today, the Huntington Townhouse hosts 5,000 events annually and Rhona has received approval to build a spa and a 244-room hotel on the site. To be catered by Rhona, of course.

"In the early days I was putting every sprig of dill on every piece of poached salmon. Now I'm much more the CEO. To be the owner of something like this is more than I could have ever dreamed. I always say that if you don't believe in miracles, just look at me. I'm the miracle CEO."

What Rhona attributes to miracles is instead a focused and tenacious execution of her vision combined with flexibility, a pioneering spirit, and old-fashioned hard work. As she and her company grew, she learned solid business principles, and, more important, carried them out.

As your business enters the growth phase, take stock by asking the same kind of questions you asked when your company was a newborn: What does the competitive environment look like now? Does your company still have the same competitive advantage? Has your business model changed? Should it change now? Can you tap into new markets or revenue streams? Could you weather unforeseen events, as Rhona did?

As your business, and its need for capital, enters a new dimension, review your business plan and the underlying business model with an eye toward updating and expanding it. Have you made plans to secure the appropriate type and amount of capital to support your company's growth? If you have outside investors, how does your plan align with their expectations? Are you keeping investors current about your plans? Are you leveraging their expertise, experience, and contacts to move the company forward? See the following Digging Deeper on capitalization strategies for your business.

DIGGING DEEPER

The ABC's of Capitalization Strategy

As your business navigates the transition from survival to expansion, you will begin to build out the infrastructure to support a more stable and sophisticated operation. This is a natural point at which to revisit your capitalization strategy. Some questions to consider:

1. *How will you fund the company's growth post start-up?* Re-evaluate the amount of capital required to support the business' growth and successfully bring it to scale. Review the types of capital available to your company and the attendant benefits and costs. Map out a capital structure that will take you furthest, fastest and at the lowest possible cost.

2. *When is the time to establish a credit relationship with a bank?* As your business grows, you are likely to need a line of credit or similar facility to finance the building of inventory and accounts receivables. Additionally, establishing a credit history with a bank is another step toward maturity for the early-stage enterprise. Remember, however, that banks are in the business of lending depositors' monies and thus are not in the business of assuming risk. Positive cash flow and/or sufficient assets to provide strong collateral coverage will be required.

3. *When is debt a good thing?* Evaluate the appropriate use of long-term debt in funding the company's growth. Weigh the pros— strategic use of leverage can boost your return on shareholder capital, and the cons—leverage can limit the company's financial flexibility and impair its ability to respond to external shocks.

4. *How should assets be funded?* Match sources and uses of funds in financing company assets. Long-term assets, *think:* property, hardware, etc. that will produce cash flow over an extended period should be funded with long-term money, *read:* equity capital or long-term debt. Short-term assets, *think:* inventory, accounts receivable, etc. that produce cash flow over a relative

(continues)

short cycle and can be funded with lines of credit and other short-term facilities.

5. *How labor intensive is your capital structure?* Each category of capital comes with its own set of requisite financial controls and reporting processes. For example, if you elect to use bank debt, you will be subject to quarterly covenant reporting and quarterly or semi-annual financial statement reporting. You must build these controls and processes into the company's operations to preclude wasting precious time and resources on the administrative aspects of the capital structure.

6. *What type of financial professional is required to manage your capital structure?* As a general rule, the sophistication and complexity of your capitalization strategy should be matched by the sophistication and expertise of the talent you hire to manage that strategy. As the business moves into expansion mode, you will likely need to relinquish your CFO hat and acquire talent that can manage the firm's funding needs on a more strategic and systematic basis.

7. *When does the capital structure move beyond a bank account to a moneymaker?* At some juncture, the business will begin to generate "excess" earnings from operations. Within the context of capital planning, consider how to optimize these earnings—i.e., to invest in short-term yield vehicles, to pay down debt, to declare a dividend to equity owners, or to reduce outside equity ownership by repurchasing shares. As the business grows, its capitalization structure can become not only a pipeline for supporting business operations but a profit center in its own right.

Courtesy etre //c

Take a fresh look at your operating team and honestly assess their strengths and weaknesses, and don't forget to look at yourself. Are team members well suited to the current demands of the company's growth while having enough potential to propel you forward? Do the company's employees share the bigger vision? Do they understand accountability, and have they taken ownership of their operating areas?

Early on, you led the charge with your boundless enthusiasm. Now, battle cries alone aren't enough. Your employees have a right and an expectation to get answers when they ask detailed questions about their retirement plans, for example. If you haven't done it before, formalize your management reporting structure and provide your employees with professional human resource policies and benefit packages.

Irene Cohen, CEO of Flexcorp Systems, has built her career on the need for human resource solutions. She gathered her wealth of knowledge by starting a staffing company, selling it, and then creating an innovative solution to the need for part-time staffing for the company who purchased her business.

Irene realized that corporations don't want to inflate their headcount with temporary workers. Instead, they prefer to adjust headcount on a real-time basis as work flows shift.

Her solution was to put temporary employees on her company's payroll, pay a portion of their benefits, and have the corporation and the temporary employee share the balance. This model gives security to the employee and maximum flexibility to the employer. Within three years, Irene left her position to start her own independent company, yet again.

"After the start-up phase, you still have to reevaluate what your core business is every minute. You've got to make sure that you don't invest in fixed costs when they can be flexible. Outsource services where you can. As you build your team, remember that the people you hired within the first two years may be perfect right now and completely out of their league two years later. You'll need to bring on people with different skill sets. Keep this in mind when you institute stock plans and other compensation programs designed to function as long-term incentives."

"While you're growing, you can and should hire the best consultants you can afford. If your $400-an-hour lawyer takes two hours to tell you what you need to know, that's a heck of a lot better than paying a $200 an hour for a junior lawyer who spends eight hours doing the research first and wastes your time in the process," Irene continues.

The growth phase of your business is an evolutionary period that can last many years. As Rhona Silver found out, you can't possibly anticipate being blindsided by unforeseen events, let alone all the other things that will happen—to the economy at large, to technology in general, or to your customer base specifically. But great leaders are great adapters and never stop learning. Not only do they continually strive to evolve their companies, they personally work to learn and grow alongside their enterprises.

See the Tool Kit on page 222 for a checklist of what business functions you should review.

Meet Carolee Friedlander. You likely know Carolee's name because you know her brand of glamorous high-end fashion jewelry, which is sold in the best department stores worldwide.

We found Carolee in her corporate headquarters, an old clapboard building off the main street in Greenwich, Connecticut. Wearing a smart black pants suit and "tons" of silver jewelry, Carolee was sitting behind a fifteen-foot-long pine farmhouse table that serves as her desk.

Greenwich is not an obvious place from which to launch a global fashion design and manufacturing company. But when Carolee started her business many years ago at her kitchen table, Greenwich was where she lived and raised her six children.

From her vantage point of thirty years of success, Carolee is well versed in the full spectrum of the phases of business: inception, survival, growth, and maturity.

"When you first start, you're a one-person show; you make it, you sell it, you ship it, you bill it, you collect the money, you do everything. You are all parts of the business enterprise wrapped into one little bundle. As you move forward, you find people who are smarter than you or who are experts in areas outside your core strengths. And you start augmenting that one little bundle with experts who can help you propel the company forward by picking up the pieces that you really don't want to do *and* probably don't have the skills to do."

When the company was independent, the execution of Carolee's vision was limited by what she could afford to spend on rolling out a retail expansion.

"In 2001, we were acquired by Retail Brand Alliance, a corporation that owns Brooks Brothers, Adrian, Casual Corner, and now Carolee, which is managed by me. We continue to operate day-to-day the same way we always have, with one important exception. We have opened fifteen Carolee retail stores and are on track to open many more. Our expansion plans were always geared toward our own retail. Being acquired has allowed me to take my vision for my company to the next level—something that would have been difficult to do on my own because I didn't have the financial or human infrastructure to do it."

Being acquired allowed Carolee to realize a handsome return on her lifetime of investment in the business. Yet she continues to play a key role in leading the company while retaining "the fun parts of her job": creativity, marketing, and sales. Carolee remains passionate about her work even after thirty years. "I've had a great time through business. I've learned so much and I've been given a lot, too. It's been a tremendous ride and it's still continuing."

The growth phase of a business leads many entrepreneurs to another stage in their personal growth and development, one that can play out in various ways.

You begin with a passion for an idea and build a business around it. You prove your critics wrong and your company thrives; but somehow, after all these years, the thrill is gone. You miss the hands-on experience. Being trotted out to close a big sale just doesn't feel as good as the buzz you get when steering your company along the razor's edge.

Lynn Lewis is a case in point. She's a fabulous baker who's never happier than when she's up to her elbows in flour. She began selling her homemade breads, cakes, and pies to a few restaurants. As word spread, she could hardly keep up with demand. She purchased her own facility, installed several ovens, hired a staff, and soon was servicing the city's top restaurants.

Then Lynn opened her first retail location. For a while, everything was great. But she was spending all her time hiring people to bake the goods and ordering the flour to make the goods. Months were flying by where she had no real contact with the products she loved to create.

Lynn recognized that she was not the one to continue to grow the business because her passion was not in running a company, but rather in the satisfaction of creating and baking. She found a partner and sold half the company to her. Now, someone else runs the business while she does what she loves as "Baker-in-Chief." Like Carolee, Lynn wanted to keep the "fun parts of her job."

For Barbara Corcoran, a powerhouse entrepreneur whose New York company nets $4 billion in revenues, the growth stage of her company involved delegating even the parts of the job she loved. Barbara is well known as a genius at branding, and her short blond hair and bright red suits are integral to her company's image. She has long capitalized on her talent and personal flair with what she calls "grandstanding and gimmickry" to draw positive media attention. The result: Her company's sales took off like a rocket.

Unlike most entrepreneurs, Barbara had an exit strategy in mind when she started her business. She thought that she might one day want to leave her full-time career for a part-time career and a full-time family. To do that, she knew she'd have to learn to delegate right from the beginning. "Whenever I opened a new office or set up a new department, I'd think, 'How would this operate if I weren't here?' It was easy to give up the parts of my job that I didn't love to do. The really hard part for me was when I had to start delegating areas that I think I'm phenomenal at—public relations and advertising."

Barbara admits to being a control freak, but feels that anyone worth her salt in any management role has to control the business so that, as the company heads down the road, everybody marches along.

"For me, the downside of being a control freak was that it was very hard for me to start delegating in areas where I believed that nobody could do it better than me. It was such baloney, but I really believed in my own unique gifts. I remember when I put in a public relations director who operated for the first year as an extension of me, unlike the heads of other departments that I just gave away. And once I put in an advertising manager, and for a full year, she, too, was operating as an extension of me."

Barbara admits that she was looking for perfection by trying to clone herself. She laughs at what she knows was a mistake:

My business was not moving ahead because I was in the way. The realization dawned: "There is an enemy. Oops, it's me." It took me a good long while to come up with what I now consider the golden rule: "The job done 80 percent as well as you could do it is good enough." From then on, I was able to delegate advertising and PR just like other pieces of the business. I learned to say, "Call me if you have a problem; if you run into a roadblock or something's stalling, then I want to know about it. Otherwise, you don't have to give me a report. You don't have to check with me. You don't have to even say good morning when you see me. But *do* call me if you have a problem."

People will go to the ends of the earth rather than admit that they can't do something you believe they can do. And, you know what? No one in advertising or in public relations called me—and there, I really thought I'd probably get even a few calls. It's funny now, but at the time it was a little bit unnerving because I saw my gifts as indispensable. I really didn't think I could be replaced, honestly. And I have been. The joke is on me. I became an excellent delegator. And I've never had a problem delegating anything again.

Another part of the phenomenal growth of Barbara's company had to do with her real feel for hiring people. "When I was traveling around, I would constantly interview people, whether it was the store clerk or the guy on the corner, just by asking some questions and getting them to talk. And I would ask myself, 'How could I use this person in my company?' I gave out my card and constantly offered starter jobs in my firm. When these spot interviewees came in for appointments, I once more turned a high-intensity beam onto them and tried to figure out where their strengths would apply to my business. Then I would create jobs around them."

We often say, "Hire for attitude, train for skills," and that's exactly what Barbara did. Her business was growing geometrically. Her people were stretching, doing several jobs until they no longer had the capacity to keep so many balls in the air. Barbara thought ahead and was able to find and hire good people in advance of the open positions.

Barbara also used her instincts and her emotions as a guideline for hiring and promotion: "When people came in for an interview, I followed the old saying, 'Ignore what they tell you and listen to the music.' When I followed my instinct, my hires were golden." Nine out of ten times, contrary to conventional wisdom, Barbara put sales people in management roles. She says, "I know that sales people can't respect management who haven't been in the trenches." What could be called "women's intuition" has been borne out by Barbara's success.

· · · ·

For many entrepreneurs, the prize is not just in succeeding in business but in finding and expressing themselves. As your company grows, it's important to stay in touch with your passion and remain true to where your interests lie. If the growth of the business leads you away from your natural interests, you may discover that it's time to rethink your role as CEO. As you move through the growth, it's wise to have a "plan B" in mind so you can decide to transition either out of the company or into another role, if appropriate.

Whether it's your decision or that of your shareholders, it's not unusual for a company to grow beyond the founder's desire or ability to move the vision forward.

If you've raised significant funding from outside investors, there is a high likelihood that ultimately you will be replaced as CEO. Investors often want chief executives with successful track records in building growth companies. This can be an awkward, unhappy, and unsettling reality for a founder; but if you recognize and acknowledge the rationale, you can make a major contribution in the selection of your successor and the execution of a transition.

Leaving the helm as CEO is perhaps one of the most meaningful, and most difficult, decisions you'll ever make. The more positively and proactively you engage in the transition, the greater the likelihood that you'll continue to have a meaningful role as the company moves forward. And, like so many entrepreneurs who love the process of turning a passion into a business, before you know it you may find yourself starting up a whole new business again.

DIGGING DEEPER

Exiting the CEO Scene

There may come a time, particularly if your company is funded by outside investors, when you will no longer continue in the role of CEO. Who reaches this conclusion, who ultimately makes the decision, what specific circumstances drive the change, and how you react to the situation all factor into your opportunity to play an ongoing role in the company. Here are two typical scenarios that represent opposite ends of a spectrum. Both are extremes and neither by definition good or bad.

- You founded the company, grew it organically with little outside money. You love what you do, love being the boss, and will work until you alone make the decision to leave, which you don't envision happening in your lifetime.

(continues)

- As founder, you took the company through many difficult days from inception through survival through raising capital. You now have a professional board whose first official act is to remove you in favor of an outsider.

The CEO must not only set the vision for the company but also construct a viable strategy to execute that vision. Clearly, one of the most important tasks is the honest assessment of skills required to lead the company forward at any particular juncture. Taking a proactive approach to this assessment, coupled with a personal reality check, will help you reach an appropriate outcome that will serve the needs of multiple constituents: the company, its employees, its investors, and you.

- You decide the company would be best served by hiring a new CEO either because your day-to-day activities no longer reflect how you want to spend your time or they are less suited to the skills you used to start the company. You initiate the search, and help screen, select, and transition your replacement. You identify a different role in the company for yourself. Or you decide to exit the company but perhaps retain a seat on the board. Or you decide to start another company.
- You find another company to acquire yours. You decide to stay on with the new company, typically running the same business you just sold. After all, who knows it better than its founder? You may take on another role with the new company or remain on the board of the combined companies without filling an operating role. Alternatively, you cash out and leave the business altogether.
- You're happy running your company and you believe you have the requisite skills to do so. Others, the board in particular, disagree. After failing to convince them, you choose not to help with a transition and are forced out. Typically, you and the board

(continues)

will agree on the "party line" before your departure. Remember that you hurt only yourself by deviating from it. When you find yourself bruised from an experience that you deem has ended badly, take the time to grieve and work through your feelings of anger and betrayal; then move forward. Business requires positive momentum. Take the time to regain that before making major decisions about your future.

As you continue your entrepreneurial journey or begin another one, it's important to remember that no one achieves success on her own. Remember to thank your employees, because it was their personal sacrifices, too, that helped the company survive and grow. Thank your investors who believed in you during the roller-coaster ride of the early days. Thank your customers for providing the revenues to keep you afloat; and thank your vendors, especially those who waited patiently for overdue payments.

Recognize that you have already influenced your community in myriad ways. You've produced needed goods and services. You've created economic benefits for the community at large through job creation and capital investment. Recognize that you now have the opportunity to share your wealth and benefit your community. Research shows that business owners, in general, are more philanthropic than the average person. Women business owners are particularly so.

Along with the privileges of success, it is important to recognize your responsibility as a businesswoman to stand tall in the community, to act ethically, and to reach a hand out to those coming up behind you. By building a viable enterprise, you've learned from your mistakes and can pass that learning on to others. You have the opportunity to inspire by example and, without even knowing it, you may fire the imagination of another who aspires to fulfill her own dream.

We hope you'll meet with, advise, and encourage those budding entrepreneurs who are now in the same situation you are in or were once in. They long for advice and encouragement. Your mentoring, coaching, and support will be one of the most valuable contributions you can make to growing the Old Girls' Network. Each of us represents a single star in this vast universe of women. By connecting with each other, we continually form and shape new and exciting constellations.

Since we gathered at the "Breakfast for Champions," we have thought long and hard about our own journeys and, by extension, the exciting adventure that you are now considering.

Some of you may have decided that starting a business of your own is more of a commitment than you want to undertake. If so, we're glad that we were able to save you time and money so that you can now effectively redirect your talents and energy.

Others of you may have underlined passages in this book, dog-eared pages, and made up a contact list as the foundation of a network of your own. Welcome to the club. We hope that we've been able to throw a bright light on the thrilling and sometimes scary journey to becoming an entrepreneur.

Writing this book has been a rare and rewarding privilege. It's our way of saying thank you to the people who have taught us and funded our dreams.

This book is also our way of connecting with you and your dream. We have an idea that one day you'll be the featured speaker at a power breakfast, a role model with an electric presence as you take the podium. It's our fondest hope that we'll be in the audience that day watching from the front row and applauding you and the grand success of your entrepreneurial dream.

WHAT YOU NEED TO KNOW

- When all appears to be stable and moving along smoothly, don't get comfortable. Expect the unexpected.
- Review your business plan periodically; make sure your underlying business model is sound and your capital needs are accounted for. Undercapitalization can kill even the soundest of plans.
- Be prepared to give up the reins in areas of the business you don't love. Be prepared to give up the reins in areas of the business you *do* love.
- Establish time frames for periodic review of your employees to ensure your team is qualified to move forward. Be brutally honest and make cuts if needed.
- Review your professional service providers, especially legal, accounting, and insurance. If you haven't switched to a recognized firm from a "one-person show," now is the time to do so. And don't skimp on professionals. The adage "You get what you pay for" is a truism.
- Review your technology, both hardware and software, including service contracts and hosting providers. As you grow, use your leverage to renegotiate better terms—or you may decide to outsource certain components of your technology.
- As well as your company may be operating "casually" with no formal structure, now is the time to formalize your management reporting structure. Create and circu-

late your HR policies and provide your employees with competitive benefits.

- Learn to delegate early on. It will enable your company to grow and will put you at a strategic advantage if you decide to sell.
- If necessary for the business, pass the CEO baton gracefully. It may be painful; however, no challenge presents itself without a gift in its hand.
- People are your most important asset. Hire for attitude, train for skills, and always trust your instincts. Remember to recognize and reward those who will be part of your future, visibly and sincerely.
- Most of all, know that you are a part of the network. Give back to others and to your community. Your contribution as a mentor and role model is priceless.

ACKNOWLEDGMENTS

We would like to give special thanks to Paula E. Chauncey, one of the original architects and authors of the book, and one of the founders of 8 Wings Enterprises LLC for her contributions. Paula has launched her new business, être llc, standing as a prime example of the Old Girls' Network and its strength in connecting women with the knowledge, expertise, and resources to forge new ground with entrepreneurial enterprises.

It is too simplistic to say a book is written. Rather, it is created. The final manuscript of *The Old Girls' Network* represents the work of many. To these remarkable people we offer our thanks and acknowledgment. We are grateful for their enthusiastic support and feel privileged to have had the opportunity to benefit from so many insightful and generous people.

It is only fitting that a book about entrepreneurs and business builders acknowledge those who were vital contributors to its creation. We would like to thank the many women who graciously contributed their time and stories so that these pages could be written. We offer special thanks to all the entrepreneurs who shared their insights. We list them in a separate section at the end of the book with information on their companies. If you are interested in learning more, please visit their Web sites; better yet, support them with your business.

We also offer deep thanks and gratitude to the many wonderful people, peers, and colleagues who supported us all the way through. We are lucky to have our own "Old Girls' Network" populated with women who inspire us, motivate us, and support us. We are especially grateful for the wisdom and friendships of Candy Brush, Trish Costello, Linda Kanner, Ann Kaplan, Ilene Lang, Sheryl Marshall, Lore McGovern, Amy Millman, Jill Preotle, Courtney Price, June Rokoff, and Andrea Silbert.

Betsy Lerner at The Gernert Company has been not just an agent but a key member of our team. She believed in us from the beginning and set the standard from the time she said "yes" over lunch at Le Colonial. She has consistently and proactively provided sound advice on all aspects of the content, the writing, the design, and the positioning of the book.

Marnie Cochran, our editor extraordinaire at Basic Books, has been our champion all along the way. We especially appreciate her expertise, commitment, and enthusiasm as she guided our roller-coaster ride of bringing this book to market.

We were fortunate to work with a gifted collaborative writer, Maxine Paetro. A great storyteller and a constant source of energy, Max has the uncanny ability to find the unique angle, the nontraditional perspective. She is a writer with special talent who helped give a cohesive voice to our writing. And to Annie Post and Peter Hillyer for their early efforts in helping us get started.

Richard Whiteley, CEO of The Whiteley Group, best-selling author, international consultant, and Sharon's husband, has been at our side from day one, guiding us as an additional pair of wings. We benefited immensely from his quiet wisdom, active coaching, cool head, and sincere interest in our project and in us as people. He was there for us all the way: facilitating the first brainstorming session in the Berkshires, guiding us through the vicissitudes of our unaccustomed and sometimes uncomfortable roles as writers, and adding his final superb edits to our submitted manuscript. We are grateful for his unflagging support as we created a book we hope can make a significant difference for individuals from all walks of life.

Finally, we would like to acknowledge each other. We are especially grateful that we share such commonality of purpose and similar philosophies and values. As partners in this endeavor, we have fully come to understand and appreciate the true meaning of the term "collaboration." Whether hammering out the premise, organizing chapters, interviewing entrepreneurs, or writing about a new idea, our willingness to assert our views and keep our minds open formed the bedrock upon which this book was created. When one of us was overextended with other commitments, the others unfailingly stepped in and picked up the slack. When one was a little discouraged, the others picked up her spirits. While we have learned many lessons through the work underlying this book, we have learned equally powerful lessons as a result of the quality of our partnership.

Sharon Whiteley

Kathy Elliott

Connie Duckworth

Boston

2003

TOOL KIT FOR
THE OLD GIRLS' NETWORK

The tools that follow have been specifically created to help you adopt and apply the concepts presented in this book to your own unique situation. Using these assessments, quizzes, and templates, as well as reading the reference material, will help you derive the most benefit from this book.

To get the most out of this Tool Kit, we suggest you review the total list that follows and then select those tools that relate to an area you wish to explore or improve. Some of the inclusions may not be relevant to your specific endeavor at this time, but maybe they will in the future. You will find sample legal documents, templates for presentations, assessment exercises, and planning frameworks for different phases of your business. An important caveat: The sample legal documents are shown for illustrative purposes only. Do not use them without consulting your attorney.

After completing the work prescribed by the tools you have chosen, you may wish to use the last one, the Personal Development Plan. This is designed especially to help you convert what you have learned into concrete action plans that will guide you to achieve the results you want.

Good luck.

TOOL KIT ITEMS

173

CHAPTER 2

THE LEGAL FORMS OF BUSINESS OWNERSHIP

The following section is not intended to be a complete discussion of all the issues that should be considered when setting up your company; rather, it highlights the importance of this decision. Tax ramifications and liability protection of owners are the key factors to consider when deciding which entity type to choose for your business. Choosing the most appropriate structure requires some long-range planning about the type of business you will ultimately create. You may decide initially to structure your business in a simple form. Growth may require you to change your company's status to a different type of entity as you bring on more employees or decide that you want to raise outside capital.

There are five basic types of ownership structures:

1. Sole Proprietorship
2. Partnership
3. LLC (Limited Liability Company)
4. S Corporation
5. C Corporation

- If you plan to stay small and simple, a sole proprietorship or partnership may be all you require. But be aware that you will be personally responsible for any debts the business incurs.
- If you plan to service customers in a commercial establishment, you should at the very least consider an LLC to protect you from liabilities that may occur during the normal course of doing business.
- Both S and C Corporations have stipulations around the number and type of investors you may solicit and the ability to retain profits to fund corporate growth. Both require formal corporate bylaws and a board of directors, but they differ distinctly on tax treatments of profits.
- In certain circumstances, it may be problematic to go from an S Corporation to a C Corporation.

There are different costs associated with setting up each structure. Federal and state laws come into play when making this decision. It is especially important to consult with an attorney who specializes in new business formation. Working with an accountant is imperative for filing the appropriate tax forms and maximizing opportunities for tax deductions and other cost savings.

CAN YOU TURN YOUR PASSION INTO A BUSINESS? (PART 1)

It is possible to translate almost any personal passion or hobby into a business idea, even if you've never thought of it that way. In the following framework, we use the example of gardening, which is America's favorite hobby, to help you think through this process. In Step 1, fill in your hobby or strength that you could turn into a business.

In Step 2, it is important to identify the specific aspect of your hobby that truly excites you. Brainstorm about the many possible businesses that relate to this particular aspect or characteristic in Step 3. At this point, the sky's the limit. Don't limit your imagination. In Step 4, you construct a list of your personal assets—your skills, talents and experiences—that could equip you to pursue the particular business that excites you. Step 5 helps you understand the differences between starting your own business and joining an existing enterprise. In Step 6, write down any and all ideas that come to mind.

This framework can also be used to explore a particular area of expertise or technical knowledge that you possess and want to build a business around, for example, marketing or sales experience, or software development expertise.

You should save your work on paper for the next part of this exercise, Part II.

Step 1: What are you passionate about?

Answer _____

e.g. Gardening

Step 2: What are the specific elements that you most enjoy or excel at?

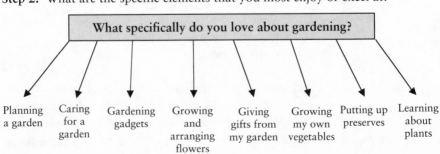

Your answer here: _____

e.g. Gardening gadgets, growing my own vegetables

Step 3: Construct a list of business options

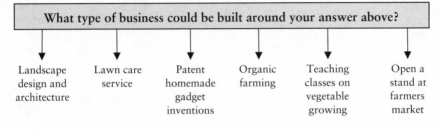

What type of business could be built around your answer above?					
Landscape design and architecture	Lawn care service	Patent homemade gadget inventions	Organic farming	Teaching classes on vegetable growing	Open a stand at farmers market

What type of business can you envision?

Your answer here: _____

e.g. Organic lawn care service or farming

Step 4: Your personal asset inventory

What personal strengths, skills and experience would you bring to the business?

Map your personal assets to the options you chose above:

List your personal strengths/assets experience:

_____
_____
_____
_____

List what is required for the business:

_____
_____
_____

e.g. good with people
knowledge of organic farming
experience working at farm stand

Step 5: Should you start your own business or join an existing company?

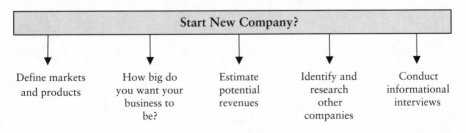

Start New Company?				
Define markets and products	How big do you want your business to be?	Estimate potential revenues	Identify and research other companies	Conduct informational interviews

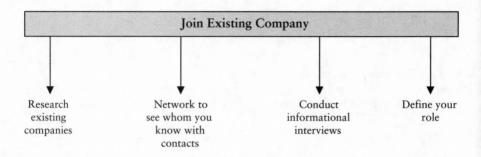

Step 6: Brainstorm on your business idea and steps you'll take to make it happen:

Your business idea: _____

_____

_____

_____

_____

CHAPTER 3

CAN YOU TURN YOUR PASSION INTO A BUSINESS? (PART 2): THE REAL, WIN, WORTH EXCERCISE

In Part 1 of this exercise, you matched your specific passion with an idea for a business that suits your personality and skill set. Now is the time to test systematically whether this potential opportunity has the legs to become a real business—whether it can produce the kind of results you desire. It may help to work through this exercise using the Competitive Analysis Tool Kit item that can help you get a start on finding out more about the business area you have chosen.

This type of reality check is important to do early on before you spend inordinate amounts of time, effort, and money pursuing a dream that may not pan out. If you find out that your original idea doesn't hold up to this careful scrutiny, don't be discouraged. Go back to Part 1 and start again.

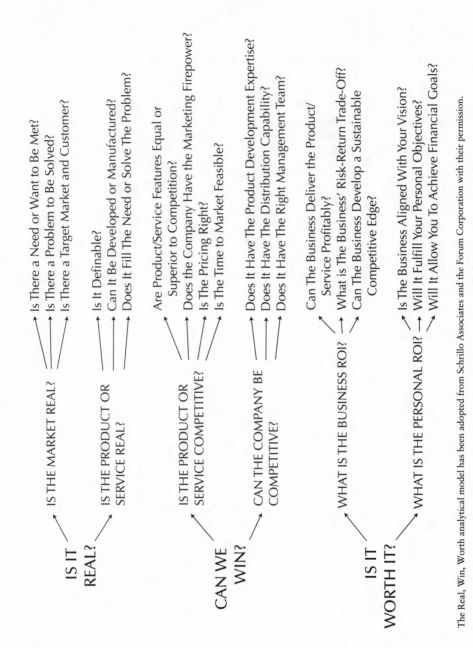

IS IT REAL?

IS THE MARKET REAL? → Is There a Need or Want to Be Met?
→ Is There a Problem to Be Solved?
→ Is There a Target Market and Customer?

IS THE PRODUCT OR SERVICE REAL? → Is It Definable?
→ Can It Be Developed or Manufactured?
→ Does It Fill The Need or Solve The Problem?

CAN WE WIN?

IS THE PRODUCT OR SERVICE COMPETITIVE? → Are Product/Service Features Equal or Superior to Competition?
→ Does the Company Have the Marketing Firepower?
→ Is The Pricing Right?
→ Is The Time to Market Feasible?

CAN THE COMPANY BE COMPETITIVE? → Does It Have The Product Development Expertise?
→ Does It Have The Distribution Capability?
→ Does It Have The Right Management Team?

IS IT WORTH IT?

WHAT IS THE BUSINESS ROI? → Can The Business Deliver the Product/ Service Profitably?
→ What is The Business' Risk-Return Trade-Off?
→ Can The Business Develop a Sustainable Competitive Edge?

WHAT IS THE PERSONAL ROI? → Is The Business Aligned With Your Vision?
→ Will It Fulfill Your Personal Objectives?
→ Will It Allow You To Achieve Financial Goals?

The Real, Win, Worth analytical model has been adopted from Schrillo Associates and the Forum Corporation with their permission.

OUTLINE FOR COMPETITIVE ANALYSIS

To compete successfully and to create a sustainable competitive advantage for your company, you must develop a sense of the competitive landscape for your industry and where your company fits into it. This is particularly important when talking to potential investors, and it will prevent you from making the classic entrepreneurial mistake of stating, "And we have no competition!"

These are the basic issues to address:

- Define your target market.
- How large is the market (in dollars)?
- Drill down to your specific niche or segment within the target market; define its size and the revenue opportunity it represents.
- How fast is the market growing overall, and in your designated segment?
- Is your arena growing faster/slower, and why?
- What is the basis for competing in the market, e.g. price, technology, ease of use, change in fashion, or consumer use patterns?
- What are the profitability characteristics of the industry? Is it a high-margined business, or driven by high volumes at low margins?
- Is it capital intensive? labor intensive?
- Define the market's seasonality and cyclicality attributes.
- Identify your targeted customers, their profile, and the size of their budgets directed to your product. How will you get to your ideal customer?
- Who are the ultimate decision makers and influencers, i.e., CFO, CTO, Head of Sales, etc., and what is the decisionmaking cycle? In a consumer business, who is the ultimate purchaser and how do they make decisions?
- Identify your competitors, both direct and indirect.
- Define your sources of sustainable competitive advantages and indicate whether they are proprietary (e.g., specialized technology).

It is important to understand your competitors' positions in the market and your strengths and weaknesses relative to alternatives.

Where to get competitive and industry information:

- Commerce Department data which can be found online or at local libraries.
- 10-K and other required financial filings of your competitors (See Edgar Online, and the Web sites, and financial information of your competitors)
- Industry trade association data (Check the Yellow Pages, do a Google search for your industry or product. (www.google.com))
- Industry publications (many can be subscribed to online at no charge)
- Proprietary research sources such as Gartner Group, Forrester Research
- Business colleagues, associates, friends, etc., who can point you in the direction of information sources and resources.
- Business magazines
- North American Industry Classifications (www.naics.com)
- Online research such as www.usdata.com
- Field research. Talk to potential customers, visit, if possible, similar businesses, decide who you would want to model your company on.

As you conduct your research, focus on the following questions: Why will my company succeed? What are the critical factors that will determine its success?

OUTLINE FOR AN EXECUTIVE SUMMARY AND BUSINESS PLAN

An Executive Summary is an introductory document used to explain your business and open the door to investors and other parties for more detailed discussions. The Executive Summary runs 2 – 4 pages long. A Business Plan builds on this outline, but in much greater detail, and usually runs 20–25 pages long. There can be many variations on formats, so ask around to see copies of actual documents. And oftentimes the sequence of material is presented in a different order to highlight the strengths of the company and its management. Whether you plan on raising outside capital or not, this is a very worthwhile exercise to undertake and will help you to understand your product and your competition. Make sure your company name, your name and contact information is included and clearly displayed.

I. **Company Description and Product Detail**
   A. Describe your product or service
   B. Why is it unique, or better, cheaper, or faster
   C. Why will you be a market leader
   D. How the product addresses your customer's needs or solves a particular problem
   E. Describe the stage of your company's development, i.e., concept stage, prototype, launch

II. **Description of your Market**
   A. Describe the target market for your company's product or service
   B. Drill down to the specific segment within the market that you are targeting
   C. How large is the market segment; how fast is it growing and what factors drive this growth
   D. Project a realistic estimate of what share of the market you capture
   E. Provide detail on your customer base: who, how many, how they make purchasing decisions

III. **Competitive Landscape**
   A. What is your competitive advantage, i.e., proprietary technology, new design, better pricing
   B. Are there barriers to entry
   C. How your product differs from the competition and why

IV. **Revenue Model and Assumptions**
   A. How you make money
   B. Pricing strategy and defensibility
   C. Costs to develop product and bring to market
   D. Minimum of 3 year projection; maximum to 5 years for revenue, expenses and profit
   E. When will you achieve break-even, cash flow positive positions

V. **Sales and Marketing Strategy**
   A. Strategy for taking product to market; how your product will be positioned
   B. Distribution plans, i.e., direct sales, distributors, strategic partnering
   C. Implementation plans and timetable

TOOL KIT

VI. Management Team

A. Why you are the management team to build this company

B. Brief bios and profiles of yourself and other key members of your management team

C. Highlight specific experience that lends itself to the enterprise

VII. Financing Details

A. How your company has funded itself to date. Description of outside capital raised, if any

B. What milestones have you achieved to date

C. How much capital are you looking to raise, and brief description of the offering, i.e. debt or equity. Don't put a dollar value on valuation in these documents

D. How you will spend the new capital you raise, i.e. sales & marketing, product development, technical support

E. Exit strategy

SAMPLE EXECUTIVE SUMMARY

Executive Summary for 600 lb gorillas, Inc.

The Company: 600 lb gorillas™ was founded in February 1999 and is based in Wrentham, Massachusetts. The company manufactures and sells premium frozen cookie dough, for resale, to more than 685 supermarkets in Massachusetts, Rhode Island, and Connecticut and 100 additional all natural stores throughout and beyond New England. 600 lb gorillas is currently being tested in club stores as a precursor to being granted shelfspace approval. The company is certified by the Woman's Business Enterprise National Council (WBENC).

The Product: 600 lb gorillas cookie dough is a premium formulation of all natural ingredients. The company's cookie dough is pre-formed into ready-to-bake "dough balls" and currently sold in four flavors: Chunky Chocolate Chip, Oatmeal Raisin with White Chocolate, Peanut Butter with Milk Chocolate, and Pecan with Chocolate Chunk. These are sold in boxes of twelve (18 oz.) through the freezer case of supermarkets and natural foods stores. A professional marketing firm was used to create an out-of-step package design and an eye-catching logo. The packaging has won an American Graphics Design Award.

Business Model: The cookie formulations are developed and tested by the company. The product is manufactured and shipped to distributors by a contract manufacturer (Skychef International, formerly Pennant Foods). Current distributors include United Natural, SuperValu, and C&S Wholesale. Johnson O'Hare Company and Eclipse Sales and Marketing provide the sales service to the retail accounts delivered to by these distributors. Consumer promotion efforts—including radio and billboard advertising, in-store sampling, and PR—are used to drive awareness, trial, and repeat purchase.

The Market: According to Nielsen and IRI data, total annual retail sales of cookies in the United States are about $4.6 billion, which translates to approximately $3.7 billion at wholesale. This figure is only for packaged cookie products (including ready-to-bake dough) sold through supermarkets, and therefore does not include in-store bakery cookies, cookies baked from scratch, or cookies sold through a wide range of other trade channels such as drug stores, convenience stores, club stores, and independent bakeries. Of the estimated $4.6 billion sold through supermarkets, approximately $376 million are sold as refrigerated cookie/brownie dough. Management believes that *frozen* cookie dough will eventually capture 20 percent of this market, as well as drive incremental sales for the category as a whole, resulting in a frozen cookie dough market of $80 million at wholesale within from three to five years.

Competition: There are three other companies that currently sell frozen pre-portioned dough balls at retail: Pillsbury, English Bay, and Mrs. Fields. The latter two can only be found in outlets other than supermarkets in the New England area, and are not supported by marketing/advertising. The Pillsbury product is out new this year (2003). Preliminary sales show that the launch of this product is helping sales of 600 lb gorillas, as it is generating awareness for the category and driving consumers to this section of the grocery freezer case.

600 lb gorillas also competes with mass-marketed refrigerated cookie dough, a market dominated by Nestle and Pillsbury, as well as with other snack foods, ice cream, and specialty baked goods found in the freezer, dairy, and bakery departments of the supermarket.

600 lb gorillas offers a much higher quality, better-tasting alternative to the Pillsbury and Nestle products above. They are also "all natural" and meet the highest standards in the all-natural specialty market. As the premium product in the category, 600 lb gorillas are able to command a pre-

mium price ($3.99 for 18 ounces vs. $3.29 for 20 ounces for competitive products).

Sales: The sales below are forecast assuming a capital investment of $XXX. A concentrated club store effort was begun in 2002. By the end of 2003, we estimate product placement in X% of club store outlets and sales of $$. (Note: We did not publish actual sales and market share forecasts for competitive reasons.)

	Year 1	Year 2	Year 3	Year 4
Sales	$xxx,xxx	$x,xxx,xxx	$x,xxx,xxx	$xx,xxx,xxx
Gross Profit	$xxx,xxx	$x,xxx,xxx	$x,xxx,xxx	$xx,xxx,xxx
Net Profit	$(xxx,xxx)	$xx,xxx	$x,xxx,xxx	$x,xxx,xxx

Management Team

Paula White
President/Cofounder, 600 lb gorillas, Inc.
Before founding 600 lb gorillas, Inc., in 1999, Paula worked as a plastics engineer designing and manufacturing medical devices for Guidant Corporation and Boston Scientific. She graduated Magna Cum Laude from the University of Lowell with a BS in plastics engineering. Paula is currently responsible for all day-to-day aspects of the business, including sales, marketing, raising capital, publicity, customer service, and bookkeeping.

Chris White
CEO/Cofounder, 600 lb gorillas, Inc.
Chris is currently working full-time as a civil engineer and works part-time evenings and weekends on the manufacturing coordination, product development and financials for 600 lb gorillas, as well as making public appearances as the "600 lb gorilla." He is a graduate of the University of Lowell with a BS in civil engineering.

Mr. John Doe
Board of Advisors, 600 lb gorillas, Inc.
Retired executive vice president of Mega Supermarkets and Big Market. During his thirty-five-year career, he held positions in marketing, procurement, merchandising, operations, corporate development, and board director. He is a past chairman of the ABC Food Association and was recently inducted into its Hall of Fame. He is currently chairman of XXX

and provides board advisory and consulting service to food industry companies.

Mr. John Smith
Board of Advisors, 600 lb gorillas, Inc.
Principal, XYZ Management, Inc.; former marketing director for Large Super Chain; former owner, founder, and CEO of large dairy product company. Joint venture partner of major yogurt company. Founder of XXX yogurt in the United States, which was sold to General Mills. He is an international corporate development consultant and is on the board of several successful food companies, including XXX Yogurt.

In addition to the advisors listed above, 600 lb gorillas has built an impressive network of informal advisors who provide continued support and networking contacts. (Note: We have disguised the name of advisors.)

Customers: Our existing customers include Stop & Shop, Star Market/Shaw's, Big Y, Foodmart/A&P, Victory Markets, Roche Bros., Bread & Circus, Wild Oats, Ro-Jacks, Trucchis, and Hannaford Bros.

Our plan is to achieve 100 percent distribution in the northeast market (approximately 650 supermarkets and 200 natural food stores) by the end of 2002. Then in 2003 to expand beyond New England to a target of 1,700 supermarket accounts, 500 natural food stores, and into club stores. By completion of 2004, we plan to have 600 lb gorillas available to consumers in more than 4,500 outlets.

Capital Investment

Funding: The company is currently funded by an SBA-guaranteed seven-year loan for $120,000 from Eastern Bank, $100,000 founder paid-in capital, and $94,000 from angel investors. The company is seeking $750,000 from a combination of angel investors ($500,000) and bank funding ($250,000) to grow and expand the company. The $750,000 will be used for working capital and targeted marketing campaigns in New England as well as for expansion into new markets.

Exit Strategy: With broad national distribution, we are likely to become an acquisition target by one of our large competitors. The market for unique brands and specialty food products is strong as evidenced by acquisitions of Smartfoods, Nantucket Nectars, and Cape Cod Potato Chips.

PROTECTING YOUR VISION:
THE NONDISCLOSURE AGREEMENT

What Is an NDA?

An NDA, or nondisclosure agreement, also known as a confidentiality agreement, is designed to protect the company's intellectual property and proprietary information from being shared with, or used by, a company's competitors *by* the parties involved in various discussions with the company. The NDA essentially binds third parties from sharing the company's information.

Depending on the nature of your business, as you grow and build strategic relationships, your company's trade secrets, confidential information and proprietary product details will increasingly be shared with a variety of outside constituents. Prospective employees, contractors, consultants, strategic partners, key customers, and investors will be interested in the details of your company's product and technology—details that will entail the disclosure of proprietary and confidential information.

Often, an early-stage company's intellectual property or proprietary approach to the market is the largest asset the company owns. You must be willing and able to disclose sensitive information to selected parties in order to foster your company's growth. Thus, you should go to great lengths to protect such information.

What Do I Need to Know About an NDA?

Bear in mind that no legal document is a surefire way to prevent malfeasance on the part of others. When possible, exclude proprietary and confidential company information from all written documents, including the executive summary and business plan. DO NOT include technical details in the materials that you distribute.

More often than not, you will find yourself engaged in discussions with companies substantially larger than your own regarding potential strategic partnerships or customer relationships. These parties will have far greater financial resources than you and it will be prohibitively expensive to enforce an NDA should it be breached. When you find yourself in situations of this nature, it is imperative to conduct thorough reference checking. Make sure that you are dealing with individuals and companies that, by reputation, will respect and honor the NDA. Finally, do not automatically sign an NDA given to you by a potential partner until you have carefully reviewed its provisions.

When Do I Use an NDA?

NDA's are common when dealing with employees, vendors, contractors, consultants, and corporations. Use an NDA with all employees who will have access to proprietary information. If an employee is vital enough to be asked to sign a noncompete agreement, chances are that she or he should be signing an NDA as well.

An NDA of a broader scope, designed to provide mutual protection, may be used when talking with potential strategic partners or large customers when it is likely that you gain access to their proprietary business information within the context of your discussions.

When Do I Not Use an NDA?

It is common practice not to request an NDA when talking with potential investors. In fact, requesting an NDA is viewed as a sign of naïveté and could end discussions before they begin. In evaluating a new technology or product, in the course of performing due diligence, investors may talk to dozens of people about the product, technology, market, competition, etc. It is very hard to conduct due diligence under the constraints of an NDA. Because it is not common practice to have a potential investor sign an NDA, reference checking again becomes imperative. It is very rare indeed for a reputable private investor or venture capital firm to misuse confidential information—after all, they depend on strong and continued flow of new deals to reach their investment objectives.

SAMPLE NONDISCLOSURE AGREEMENT

Confidentiality Agreement

CONFIDENTIALITY AGREEMENT by and between Company A Corporation, with its principal place of business at "X" (hereinafter referred to as "Company A"), and Company B, Inc. with its principal place of business at "Y" (hereinafter referred to as "Partner.")

1. "Confidential Information" means (including tangible, intangible, and oral and written) (a) any technical, or business information, designs, inventions, manufacturing technique, process, experimental work, program, software or trade secret relating to products, systems, equipment, services, sales, partner lists, research or business of the Parties, their members or subsidiaries; (b) documents

marked "Confidential"; and (c) documents, plans, prints, tapes, disks, and other material containing any of the foregoing.

2. The limitations on disclosure or use of Confidential Information shall not apply to, and the Parties shall not be liable for disclosure or use of Confidential Information if any of the following conditions exist: (a) if, prior to the receipt thereof from the other Party, it has been developed independently by the recipient party, or was lawfully known by the recipient Party; (b) if, subsequent to receipt thereof (i) it is made available to the general public, without restriction, or (ii) it has been lawfully obtained by the recipient Party from other sources, provided such source did not receive it due to a breach of an obligation of confidentiality to a third party or the parties; or (c) if it becomes generally known to the public other than pursuant to disclosure by either Company A or Partner.

3. The Parties acknowledge that they may from time to time transfer Confidential Information to each other, and therefore agree to the following with respect to Confidential Information.

(i) Not to make copies of any Confidential Information or any part without the permission of the other Party;

(ii) Not to disclose any Confidential Information or any part to others for any purpose without written consent of the other Party;

(iii) To limit dissemination of Confidential Information to the Party's employees who have a need to know and use Confidential Information for the purposes of such performance and who have been advised of and agree to the obligations and restrictions on persons receiving such information as set forth in this Agreement;

(iv) To treat Confidential Information as strictly confidential and as trade secret information, by protecting such information in the manner and subject to the same protection as the Parties treat and protect their respective proprietary information of like importance but in any event using no less than reasonable care;

(v) To disclose Confidential Information to third parties only with the prior written consent of the other Party;

(vi) To return Confidential Information and any copies thereof to the respective Party upon written request of the other Party;

(vii) Not to use Confidential Information for any purpose other than to effect the business relationship between the disclosing Party and the receiving Party.

Notwithstanding the foregoing, the recipient may disclose Confidential Information to the extent that such disclosure is required by law or court order, provided, however, that the recipient provides to the disclosing party prior written notice of such disclosure and reasonable assistance in obtaining an order protecting the Confidential Information from public disclosure.

4. The Parties acknowledge and agree that the restrictions contained in this Agreement are necessary for the protection of the business and property of both Parties, and consider them to be reasonable for such purpose. The parties agree that any breach of this Agreement may cause the other Party substantial, irreparable and irrevocable damage and therefore, in the event of such breach, the Party damaged shall be entitled to specific performance and other injunctive relief, in addition to such other remedies as may be afforded by applicable law.

5. This Agreement shall commence as of the date of the last signature to this Agreement (the "Effective Date") and shall terminate ten (10) days following receipt by a party of the other party's written notice that such party desires to terminate this Agreement. Notwithstanding termination of this Agreement for any reason, the obligations of the recipient under this Agreement with regard to a particular item of confidential information shall survive for a period of three (3) years following the date of disclosure of such particular item of confidential information.

6. This Agreement is governed by the internal substantive laws of the (applicable state), without respect to its conflict of laws principles. The waiver by one party of a breach of any provision of this Agreement by the other party shall not operate or be construed as a waiver of any subsequent breach of the same or any other provision by the other party. If any provision of this Agreement is held to be invalid, void, or unenforceable, the remaining provisions shall nevertheless continue in full force. Each of the parties hereto acknowledges that it has read this Agreement, understands it, and shall be bound by its terms. This Agreement constitutes the entire understanding of the parties with respect to its subject matter and supersedes any prior agreement or understanding, written or oral, between the parties with respect to its subject matter. This Agreement may be amended only by a writing that specifically

refers to this Agreement and is signed by duly authorized representatives of both parties. This Agreement may be signed by the parties in separate counterparts which shall together constitute one and the same agreement. Signatures transmitted via facsimile shall be valid and binding as originals.

AGREED: AGREED:

COMPANY A CORPORATION   _____

                                 ("PARTNER")

SIGNED:_____   SIGNED:_____

NAME: _____   NAME:_____

TITLE:_____   TITLE: _____

DATE: _____   DATE:_____

CHAPTER 4

MILESTONE SETTING

Milestones	Projected Completion Date	Responsible Party	Current Status
1. Design phase I prototype for initial product			
2. Select industrial design firm to assist in refining product design			
3. Define selection criteria (company size, materials quality, pricing, delivery time) for suppliers providing raw materials for product manufacturing			
4. Identify, complete due diligence on, and select raw materials suppliers. Negotiate contracts.			
5. Define selection criteria for contract manufacturing sources.			
6. Identify, complete due diligence on, and select contract manufacturers. Negotiate contracts.			
7. Identify, select and contract with packaging design firm to develop product packaging.			
8. Complete initial trial manufacturing run for product.			

CHAPTER 5

DO YOU HAVE WHAT IT TAKES TO BE AN ENTREPRENEUR?

Read each scenario (based on actual situations) described below and pick one answer that you think would most closely resemble what your immediate reaction would be. There are no "right" or "wrong" answers. Then see the end of the quiz to analyze your responses.

1. When I am confronted with criticism about the "competition" section of my business plan, I say the following to myself:
   A. "This person doesn't know what the heck they're talking about."
   B. "Yeah, but, they don't have the experience in this market that I have."
   C. "This observation makes sense, and I will think about it more and analyze the implications."

2. The local banker has met with you twice now, and wants to see more data on your monthly financial projections. You say to yourself:
   A. "If he can't see how the numbers work, I am not going to bother doing more work for him."
   B. "I'll just fudge some data, but in the meantime I'll look for someone else to give me the money."
   C. "He seems really interested, and I know just what he's looking for. I'll work on that later tonight, and I can also use these numbers to help my sales team with their budgets.

3. You are building a top-notch advisory board, and a colleague has introduced you to a former CEO of a leading technology company. You have an hour-long meeting. Here's what you come away with:
   A. "That egomaniac wants me to do all the work building this company, and then he'll try to come in and take things over."
   B. "He'd be a great fit, but I'm afraid he will overshadow me."
   C. "I can't believe I have the opportunity to have a luminary of such experience interested in joining my advisory board. I'll call my attorney right away and have him draft up the documents for this advisory board engagement."

4. Based on input from one of your angel investors, you are now considering hiring a top-notch salesperson to help get your company to the next level. You meet with a very qualified and self-assured individual and he/she is available and interested. You:

   A. Think she is arrogant, and wants a very high salary. You keep her hanging hoping she will become desperate and offer to take your job at lower pay.

   B. Really like this person's energy and drive. He would be an excellent fit, but you indicate to him you are looking to hire someone more affordable. You let him know this decision during the interview, expecting that he will probably find another opportunity soon.

   C. After the interview you envision the significant impact a salesperson of this caliber can bring to your company. The candidate is very interested in the potential of your business, however, his justified salary requirements are high. You meet with your investors and brainstorm ways to make this hire affordable.

5. You are at the early stages of building your company and have "maxed" out on your credit cards. You learn in a community college session about funding early stage companies with "family and friends'" money. A light bulb goes off. You call your rich aunt and ask whether she would like to have lunch, during which time you:

   A. Go into the meeting assuming she is gullible and knows nothing about business, so you are sure you can talk her into writing you a check right then and there.

   B. Realize that your aunt believes in supporting women with a business dream, and wants more information. But, you were not prepared for this positive a response and do not have back-up information. The lunch meeting quickly turns to your aunt lecturing you on how you "should" approach the subject. You shut down.

   C. Want to go into this meeting prepared so you call you lawyer for basic documents. You also bring your latest business plan. She is very interested and wants to go to the next step. You ask, and she agrees, to be on your advisory board.

6. Your company just landed its first big customer and you need to upgrade to a law firm that specializes in high growth/early stage companies to handle your needs. You identify the best firms, and one of your board members offers to make introductions. At this first meeting with the recommended firm, you are unexpectedly met by a junior associate, not the partner you were slated to meet with. You:

   A. Have a hard time hiding the fact that you are upset at what you envision is a slight. You spend your meeting time thinking how you will confront your big board member when the meeting is over.

   B. Appreciate the time that is being spent with you, but you only half listen to what seems like a perfunctory sales pitch.

   C. You don't want to waste this introduction so you turn the interview into an informational session. You probe the associate for insights into the firm and others, and learn what you can do to get the attention of a senior partner. You leave with new knowledge and insights.

7. After months of hard work drafting a full-blown business plan, you secure a "dry run" presentation with a local venture capital firm. Your presentation is excellent, however your audience interrupts throughout. The lead investor exits the meeting after five minutes, wishing you good luck—and "no thank you." You:

   A. Blast out of the meeting in a snit, mentally lambasting the venture capitalist for his obvious arrogance.

   B. Think that they liked your plan, but would not fund you because you are a woman.

   C. Stride confidently out of the room, draft a follow-up letter thanking the company for their valuable time and input and request a short follow-up phone meeting for additional feedback, and names of other venture firms they would recommend.

Analyzing the Results

If you answered "A" to most of these questions, you verge on obstinance. Notice how most of your responses actually put down the other person. It is clear you cannot accept criticism, and tend to deflect it back to the source it is coming from. This is a stumbling block because it may indicate that you will be unwilling to listen to customers, employees, and potential investors.

If "B" was your typical response, notice the word "but" in each answer. You suffer from the "Yeah, but . . ." syndrome and will have to work harder to keep an open mind to criticism and differentiate valid critiquing from other viewpoints. Putting together your advisory board to help interpret and respond to criticism and less-than-optimum situations is one step to take.

We like "C" answers because you see the positive side of this feedback and the possibilities in these situations. You forge ahead with an action plan. You may not always have all the answers, but your attitude will serve you well.

CHAPTER 6

SAMPLE TERM SHEET

Term Sheet Financing Document
For Proposed Private Placement
Of Series A–1 Convertible Preferred Stock
of
"Your Company," Inc.

This term sheet (the "*Term Sheet*") summarizes the basic terms and conditions on which one or more accredited investors (collectively, "*Investor*") may purchase Series A–1 Convertible Preferred Stock of *Your Company, Inc.* (the "*Company*"), a Delaware corporation (the "*Transaction*").

Pre-Money Valuation: $X
Minimum Amount of Investment: $X
Securities to be Issued: Upon receipt by the Company of all required shareholder consents, up to X shares of Series A–1 Convertible Preferred Stock (the "*Series A–1 Stock*").
Purchase Price: $.X per share (the "*Original Purchase Price*").
Capitalization of the Company: The capitalization of the Company after giving effect to the proposed investment (assuming the sale of a total of X shares of Series A–1 Stock for an aggregate amount of $X) is set forth on *Exhibit A* attached hereto.
Closing Date: The closing is expected to occur on or before _____, (year) unless extended by the Company in its sole discretion (the "*Closing Date*").
Use of Proceeds: For general working capital purposes.
Investors: Accredited investors reasonably acceptable to the Company.
Warrants: On the Closing Date, the Company shall issue to Investor a warrant to purchase a number of shares of Series A–1 Stock equal to twenty-five percent (25%) of the number of shares of Series A–1 Stock purchased by Investor on the Closing Date at a price per share equal to the Original Purchase Price (the "*Warrant*"). The Warrant shall become exercisable on the first anniversary of the Closing Date and shall expire on the sixth anniversary of the Closing Date.
Rights and Preferences of the Series A–1 Stock:
  (i) *Dividend Provisions:* The holders of Series A–1 Stock will be entitled to receive, when, if and as declared by the Board of Directors,

and in any event upon the liquidation, dissolution or winding up of the Company or the redemption of such shares of Series A–1 Stock, out of funds legally available therefore, cumulative dividends at the annual rate of $.X per share, payable in preference and priority to any payment of any dividend or distribution on, or upon redemption of, any other class or series of capital stock of the Company.

(ii) *Conversion*:   A holder of Series A–1 Stock will have the right to convert Series A–1 Stock, at the option of such holder, at any time, into shares of Common Stock. The total number of shares of Common Stock into which Series A–1 Stock may be converted initially will be determined by dividing the Original Purchase Price by the conversion price (the "*Conversion Price*"). The initial Conversion Price will be the Original Purchase Price The Conversion Price will be subject to adjustment to reflect stock dividends, stock splits, and similar events.

(iii) *Automatic Conversion*:   The Series A–1 Stock will be automatically converted into Common Stock, at the then-applicable Conversion Price upon (a) the closing of an underwritten public offering of shares of the Company at a price per share of at least $X resulting in net proceeds to the Company of at least $X (a "*Qualified Public Offering*") or (b) the written consent of the Series A–1 Majority Holders (as hereinafter defined).

(iv) *Antidilution Provisions*:   The Conversion Price of the Series A–1 Stock will be subject to proportional adjustment (i) for stock dividends, stock splits, or similar events and (ii) on a full ratchet adjustment basis to prevent dilution in the event that the Company issues additional shares of stock at a purchase price less than the applicable Conversion Price. No adjustment to the Conversion Price will occur for any issuance of additional shares at a purchase price in excess of the current Conversion Price. The Conversion Price will not be adjusted upon (a)conversion of Series A Convertible Preferred Stock (the "Series A Stock"); (b) conversion of Series A–1 Stock, (c)the issuance and sale of, or the grant of, Common Stock or options to purchase Common Stock pursuant to the Company's current or future employee incentive stock purchase or option plans, the terms of which shall be approved by the Company's Board of Directors (the "*Employee Plans*"), (d) the issuance of shares of Common Stock or warrants for Common Stock to strategic partners of the Company or in connection with bank lines of

credit, equipment lease transactions or real estate transactions, provided such issuance was approved by the Company's Board of Directors, (e) securities issued solely in consideration for the acquisition (whether by merger or otherwise) by the Company of all or
substantially all of the capital stock or assets of any other entity, or
(f) securities issued in a Qualified Public Offering (the foregoing collectively, the "*Excepted Securities*")

(v) *Liquidation Preference:*   In the event of any liquidation, dissolution, or winding up of the Company, the holders of Series A–1 Stock
will be entitled to receive, *pari passu* with the holders of the Series A
Stock (the Series A Stock and Series A–1 Stock collectively referred
to as the "Preferred Stock"), and in preference to the holders of
Common Stock and holders of any other class or series of capital
stock an amount equal to the Original Purchase Price per share, plus
any dividends accrued but unpaid on the Series A–1 Stock (the "*Liquidation Preference*"). After payment of the Liquidation Preference,
the remaining assets of the Company shall be distributed ratably to
the holders of Common Stock.

At the option of the holders of a majority of the then-outstanding
Preferred Stock (the "*Preferred Stock Majority Holders*"), a sale of
all or substantially all of the assets of the Company or a merger by
the Company with or into another entity in which a majority of the
voting control of the Company is transferred will be deemed to be a
liquidation for the purposes of the Liquidation Preference. The
Company shall provide the holders of Preferred Stock all information relating to any transaction or series of transactions that may be
deemed to be a liquidation, dissolution or winding up for purposes
of the Liquidation Preference including, but not limited to, information relating to any third-party acquirers and the terms of such
transaction or series of transactions.

(vi) *Redemption Rights*:   At the election of the holders of a majority of
the then-outstanding Series A–1 Preferred Stock (the "Series A–1
Majority"), the Company shall, on the fifth anniversary of the Clos-
ing Date and on each of the first, second and third anniversaries
thereof (each a "*Mandatory Redemption Date*"), redeem X percent
(X%) of the shares of Series A–1 Stock held by each holder of Series
A–1 Stock (such that all of the outstanding shares of Series A–1
Stock will be redeemed on the final Mandatory Redemption Date) at

a price per share equal to the Original Purchase Price, plus any accrued and unpaid dividends. To the extent that the Company may not on any such date legally redeem such Series A–1 Stock, such redemption will take place in a single transaction or a series of transactions when and as funds are legally available therefor. The Company shall not redeem any other series or class of capital stock prior to the redemption of the Series A–1 Stock; *provided, however,* that the Company may redeem the Series A Preferred contemporaneously with the Series A–1 Stock on a pro rata basis.

(vii) *Voting Rights*:   A holder of Series A–1 Stock will have the right to that number of votes equal to the number of shares of Common Stock issuable upon conversion of its Series A–1 Stock at the time the shares are voted.

(viii) *Board of Directors:*   The Board of Directors will consist of 5 persons. The stockholders shall agree to vote their shares to elect: 1 director designated by the holders of Common Stock (who shall initially be *"name,"* who shall be appointed as Chairperson of the Board), 2 directors designated by the holders of Series A Stock (one of whom shall initially be *"name"*), and 2 directors designated by the holders of Series A Stock, Series A–1 Stock and Common Stock voting together as a single class (with voting rights to be determined on an as-converted basis; one of whom shall initially be *"name,"* who shall be appointed as Vice-Chairperson of the Board).

(ix) *Protective Provisions*:   Consent of the Preferred Stock Majority Holders will be required for any action which would:

   a. change the rights, preferences, or privileges of the any series of the Preferred Stock;

   b. create any new class or series of securities which has a preference over the Preferred Stock, or offering of the Company's equity securities on a pari passu basis with the Preferred Stock;

   c. authorize the consolidation or merger of the Company or the sale of all or substantially all of the assets of the Company (a *"Sale"*);

   d. authorize the payment of dividends on shares other than the shares of Preferred Stock;

   e. require or authorize the repurchase or redemption of outstanding shares, except for repurchase of unvested shares from the Founders (as set forth below) or from employees, directors and consultants at cost, pursuant to the terms of agreements providing for the original issuance of such shares (or options to purchase such shares);

   f. amend the Company's Certificate of Incorporation or bylaws in a manner that adversely affects the rights of the holders of Preferred Stock; or

   g. increase or decrease the authorized number of directors constituting the Board of Directors.

Preemptive Rights: In the event that the Company offers any class or series of equity securities, each holder of at least X shares of Preferred Stock (each a *"Preferred Stock Major Holder"*) shall have a right of first refusal to purchase the same percentage of such additional equity securities of the Company as the percentage of Common Stock owned by such stockholder. For purposes of making such a computation, each Preferred Stock Major Holder shall be deemed to own the number of shares of Common Stock into which such Preferred Stock is at that time convertible plus the number of shares of Common Stock actually held by such Preferred Stock Major Holder, and all outstanding options and warrants will be deemed to have been exercised. Notwithstanding the foregoing, this right of first refusal shall not apply to the Excepted Securities.

This right of first refusal will terminate upon the closing of a Qualified Public Offering or upon the consummation of a Sale of the Company.

Right of First Refusal & Right of Co-Sale: If *"name"* proposes to sell all or any portion of his/her interest in the capital stock of the Company to a third party, the Company will have a right of first refusal to purchase such shares on the terms of such proposed sale. If the Company does not wish to repurchase such shares or is unable to do so in any particular instance, it will assign such right pro rata to the Preferred Stock Major Holders.

If the holders of Preferred Stock Major Holders and the Company decline to exercise their respective rights of first refusal in full, the Preferred Stock Major Holders shall have a right of co-sale to participate in such sale by *"name"* to the extent of their respective percentage ownership in the Company on a fully-diluted basis.

The right of first refusal and the right of co-sale will not apply to transfers or sales (a) to affiliates, on death, by gift to immediate family members, for estate planning purposes and the like, (b) pursuant to a Qualified Public Offering, or (c) upon a Sale of the Company. The right of first refusal and the right of co-sale will terminate upon the closing of a Qualified Public Offering or upon the consummation of a Sale of the Company.

Information Rights: The Company will furnish to all holders of Preferred Stock annual financial statements within "X" days after the end of each fiscal year. Such financial statements shall be audited if the management of the Company determines in good faith that the Company has sufficient revenues to justify the cost of such audit.

Registration Rights:

(i) *Demand Registration:*   At any time after "X" months after an initial public offering of the Company's Common Stock, if the holders of more than "X" (x%) percent of the outstanding shares of the Preferred Stock, including Common Stock issued upon conversion of the Preferred Stock (*"Registrable Securities"*), request that the Company file a registration statement to register shares of Registrable Securities, the Company will use its best efforts to cause such shares to be registered.

The Company shall not be obligated to effect more than (X) registrations under these demand right provisions and shall not be obligated to effect a registration (i) during the X day period commencing with the date of the Company's initial public offering or (ii)if it delivers notice to the holders of the Registrable Securities within X days of any registration statement for such initial public offering within X days.

(ii) *Registration on Form S–3:*   In addition to the registration rights granted above, the holders of Registrable Securities shall be entitled to unlimited demand registrations on Form S–3 or any successor Form (if available to the Company) so long as each such registered offering is not less than $X

(iii) *Piggyback Registration:*   The holders of Registrable Securities shall be entitled to "piggyback" registration rights on all registrations by the Company or any demand registrations of any other security holder of the Company subject to the right, however, of the Company and its underwriters to reduce the number of shares proposed to be registered in view of the market conditions; *provided, however,* that the shares of the investors proposed to be registered shall only be reduced (pro rata with the shares "X" Inc. proposed to be registered) after the shares proposed to be registered pursuant to the registration rights of all security holders other than the investors and "X" Inc. (including shares proposed to be registered by the Company) are first reduced completely.

(iv) *Lock-Up Provisions:* If requested by the Company and its underwriters, no holder of Registrable Securities will sell its shares for a specified period (but not to exceed X days) following the effective date of the Company's initial public offering; provided that all officers and directors of the Company are similarly bound.

(v) *Expenses:* The Company shall bear registration expenses (exclusive of underwriting discounts and commissions) of all such demand, piggyback, and S–3 registrations (including the expense of one special counsel of the selling shareholders which shall be designated by the investors).

(vi) *Termination:* The demand, piggyback and S–3 registration rights set forth above shall terminate upon the earlier of (i) five (5) years after the initial public offering of the Company's Common Stock or (ii) with respect to any individual holder of Registrable Securities, when all of such holder's shares may be sold in any 91 day period pursuant to Rule 144.

(vii) *Additional Registration Rights:* The Company will not grant any additional registration rights (except pursuant to the Company's Employee Plans) to others without the consent of the Series A–1 Majority Holders.

(viii) *Indemnification*: In connection with each registration of Registrable Securities, the Company and each holder of the Registrable Securities will indemnify each other and certain related and other parties, on customary terms and conditions, against liabilities arising under applicable securities laws for inadequate disclosure and other violations for which they are responsible.

Transaction Documents: The purchase and sale of the Series A–1 Stock will be made pursuant to a stock purchase agreement, stockholders agreement, registration rights agreement, and related documents (the *"Transaction Documents"*) which will contain, among other things, in form and substance satisfactory to counsel for Investor, appropriate representations and warranties of the Company, covenants of the Company reflecting the provisions set forth herein, such investment representations by Investor as may be required in connection with applicable federal and state securities laws, and appropriate conditions of closing.

Governing Law: The internal laws of the State of Delaware.

Conditions to Closing: The closing of the purchase and sale of the Series A–1 Stock will be conditioned upon:

a. completion of due diligence to the satisfaction of Investor;

b. execution and delivery by the Company of the Transaction Documents;

c. compliance by the Company with applicable securities laws; and

d. such other conditions as are customary for transactions of this type.

Key Man Life Insurance: The Company will maintain $X life insurance policies on the lives of _____ with proceeds payable to the Company.

Expenses: If the Closing occurs, each party shall be responsible for its respective costs and expenses incurred by it in connection with the transactions contemplated hereby.

Counsel to "Your Company" Inc.:

Term Sheet Only: Except for the Expense provision hereof, this Term Sheet is not binding and is subject to the completion of due diligence by Investor.

"YOUR COMPANY" INC.

Date: By:
Name:
Title:

INVESTOR:
Date: By:
Name:
Title:

INVESTOR:
Date:
Print Name:
Signature Page to
Series A–1 Private Placement Term Sheet

EXHIBIT A
"Your Company," Inc. Capitalization Table

(Note: You would attach the Capitalization Table which lists the amount of shares issued, to whom, and at what price.)

POWER POINT INVESTOR PRESENTATION

These are suggested generic slide titles that you can adapt to your company's specific situation and the interests of your potential investor.

I. *Who We Are . . . What We Do*
   · Description of Company—its products/services
     (Why will you be a market leader?)

II. *The "Problem"-or-The Market "Need"* (pick one)
   · Describe the problem you are solving—or the real market need you are filling

III. *Your Solution* (to problem) *or Answer* (to need)
   · Describe how your products or services solve/answer issue

IV. *The Market*
   · Overall size and rate of growth
   · Drill down to your specific market segment
   · Project your realistic market capture; rate of growth
     likely 2 slides (graphs/charts useful)

V. *Competitive Landscape*
   · List competitors (indirect & direct) and your relative position to them
   · Define what they do

VI. *Your Competitive Advantage—Differentiators*
   · Describe the differentiating benefits and features of your products/services. Why will you be a market leader?
   · Barriers to entry?
   · Barriers to exit?

VII. *What Our Customers Have to Say About Us*
   · Testimonial(s) from satisfied audience(s)
     (up to three if short)

VIII. *Business Model*
   · Describe how you make money
   · Pricing strategy and defensibility
   · Growth opportunity

IX. *Financial Projections*
   · Minimum three years; max five years (summary only)

X. *Sales and Business Development*
   · Sales & customer acquisition strategy
   · Customer retention plans

- · Strategic partnerships
- · Acquisitions
XI. *Marketing Plan*
  - · Overall Strategy
  - · Alliances/partners
  - · Initiatives to date (if any)
XII. *Our Management Team*
  - · Summary profile of senior team
  - · Highlight and emphasize relevant skills, domain expertise, track records
  - · Reference additional hires (if relevant) for future
  - · Note Advisory Board/Board of Directors (if assembled)
XIII. *Milestones*
  - · Accomplishments to date
  - · Next goal phase with specific initiatives
XIV. *Investment Opportunity*
  - · Current financing and use of funds
  - · Projected next round (note time frame, projected amount, use of funds)
XV. *Future Exit Opportunities*
  - · Strategic merger & or acquisition
  - · Roll-up
  - · IPO (market dependent)

Determine in advance the nature of each meeting that you will have with prospective investors. An initial, introductory meeting may permit enough time for ten slides. Other meetings may allow you to include more. Cull the list above to your ten most important slides so you are always prepared for an introductory meeting. Don't clutter slides with too much information.

DUE DILIGENCE CHECKLIST

If your company gets to the stage where it will be raising outside capital, having all your books and records in order will make the process that much easier, and will work in your favor. Start as early as possible to keep the most organized and complete records that you can. The time it takes up front to do so is minimal compared to the time it may take to undo things done poorly or incorrectly. Here is a comprehensive "due diligence" checklist typically used by an investor's attorney before any investment is under-taken or for the process of merger or acquisition discussions. Many of the items may apply to larger companies and may or may not be applicable for many early-stage companies. Nonetheless, the key message is to keep orga-nized and comprehensive records at *all* stages of your business.

Note: This is the legal portion of a complete due diligence. The investor will be pursuing their own due diligence on your product, competitive ad-vantage, the market, as well as references and background checks, on you and your team.

Corporate Records

- ☐ The Company's original Certificate or Articles of Incorporation (or sim-ilar document) in the jurisdiction where the Company is incorporated or registered, together with all amendments to date.
- ☐ The Company's By-laws or Articles of Association (or similar docu-ment, as applicable) for the Company, as currently in effect.
- ☐ Minutes of meetings of the Board of Directors, Executive Committee, and any other Committee of the Board of Directors and shareholders of the Company since its date of incorporation, and organization minutes and all minutes that show share authorizations (including option grants) since the date of incorporation.
- ☐ Stock transfer ledger of the Company; form of stock certificate.
- ☐ Communications to stockholders by the Company for the past five years.
- ☐ Press clippings and releases relating to the Company for the past three years.
- ☐ Applications for, and documents evidencing authority of the Company to do business as a foreign corporation in jurisdictions other than that of its incorporation.
- ☐ Stockholders' agreements, proxies, voting trusts, or similar agreements.
- ☐ Organizational chart of the Company including a list of all subsidiaries and stockholders.

Insurance

- ☐ A schedule of all insurance policies of the Company, identifying the car-rier, coverage limits, deductible amounts, renewal dates, and premiums paid.
- ☐ Detailed insurance claims history as to all such policies and a descrip-tion of self-insurance reserves.

❏ Documents and reports relating to calculations of the Company's experience ratings relating to any such policies, plus any unemployment insurance experience ratings.

Governmental Regulations and Filings

❏ Reports filed and any significant or nonroutine correspondence with any governmental authorities during the past five (5) years.

❏ Governmental licenses, permits, authorizations, approvals, etc. (including renewal dates) of the Company, together with any applications therefor.

❏ Bonds or other security posted for regulatory licenses, permits, authorizations, or approvals.

❏ Lists and records of investigations, inquiries, or inspections by governmental authorities within the past seven (7) years.

❏ Any orders of governmental authorities by which the Company or their properties or operations are bound.

Financings

❏ Documents and agreements evidencing borrowings, whether secured or unsecured, including (i) loan, credit and security agreements, promissory notes, and other evidences of indebtedness, (ii) all guarantees, whether by or on behalf of the Company, and (iii) all documents and agreements relating to industrial development bond financings.

❏ Bank and financing company letters or agreements confirming lines of credit.

❏ Documents and agreements evidencing other financing arrangements including sale and lease-back arrangements, installment purchases, conditional sales contracts, intercompany financing, etc.

❏ Correspondence with lenders (including entities committed to lend) for the last three years, including all compliance reports submitted by the Company or its independent public accountants.

❏ Documents evidencing satisfaction of indebtedness during the past three years.

❏ Loan agreements and any other documentation relating to loans or advances to, or investments in, any other person or entity and any intercompany loans, advances, or investments.

❏ Guarantees in respect of any indebtedness or any obligation of any other person.

Financial Information

☐ Audited annual financial statements for the past five years for the Company, plus auditors' work papers, planning memoranda, and attorney letters in connection therewith.

☐ Unaudited monthly and quarterly financial statements for the past five years, to the present date; monthly trial balances for the past and current year.

☐ Current operating and capital budgets, with related back-up and assumptions.

☐ Capital spending commitments and internal procedures relating thereto.

☐ Previously issued budgets/projections for the prior three years' through (year). Operating results with comparison against actual results through the current date.

☐ Changes in accounting practices during the past five years, if any, and their impacts.

☐ Summary of inventory stocked by the Company. If the Company bundles hardware with its products, assess reasonableness of inventory balances with respect to obsolescence issues.

☐ Aged accounts receivable and payables list for the Company at prior year end, and at the end of each of the first (three) quarters of the current year.

☐ Complete list of all assets with a purchase price in excess of $5,000, including description, acquisition date, cost basis, location, and depreciation life for financial and tax accounting purposes.

☐ Correspondence with outside and inside accountants regarding controls.

Taxes

☐ Foreign, state and local returns relating to income, sales, use, employment, payroll, property, or any other taxes for the past ten years.

☐ Report of adjustments and settlements by a taxing authority for the last two audit periods for all applicable taxes.

☐ Proposed taxing authority adjustments and settlements for all current audits.

☐ Notices received from, and any related communications with any taxing authorities concerning any investigation or audit of tax liabilities for the past ten years, including any liabilities or penalties assessed.

☐ Records of all FICA, FUTA, and other withholdings from employee compensation for the past five years.

- ❏ Copies of all current extensions of statutes of limitations.
- ❏ Copies of all deferred tax schedules.
- ❏ Illegal or questionable payments.
- ❏ Determination of tax versus book basis of assets; property depreciation and rates.
- ❏ Assumptions made, and worksheets used, in calculating any potential recapture amounts (e.g., depreciation, ITC and other benefit items such as bad debt reserves).

Customer Information

- ❏ Representative customer agreements and copies of all current agreements with the customers identified in Paragraph 7.2.
- ❏ List of ten largest customers for each of the past three years; list of sales to each.
- ❏ List of any customers who are governmental or quasi-governmental entities (whether federal, state, or local).
- ❏ Copy of all catalogs, product literature, advertising materials, including price lists.

Agreements

- ❏ All agreements, indentures, or other instruments that contain restrictions with respect to payment of dividends or other distributions in respect to the Company's capital stock.
- ❏ Agreements, contracts or commitments relating to capital expenditures.
- ❏ Licensing agreements, franchises, joint venture, and partnership agreements, if any.
- ❏ All interconnection agreements and leases.
- ❏ Agreements, contracts, or commitments limiting the freedom of the Company to engage in any line of business or to compete with any other person.
- ❏ Agreements, contracts, or commitments not entered into in the ordinary course of business, which involve $10,000 or more, are not cancelable without penalty within thirty days, or have a remaining term in excess of one year.
- ❏ Agreements, contracts or commitments to pay for or indemnify against the debts or liabilities of third parties.
- ❏ Principal documents relating to any acquisitions or dispositions of businesses by the Company.

❏ Contracts, agreements or arrangements between the Company and any of its directors, officers, or stockholders (or any affiliate or relatives of such directors, officers or stockholders).

❏ Contracts of the Company relating to its securities, including stock option plans and stock option agreements. Any documents pertaining to any preemptive rights outstanding with respect to any securities of the Company.

❏ Sample forms of purchase orders.

❏ Distribution Agreements, if any.

❏ List of, and copies of, documents relating to the Company's or stockholders' interests in any entity that is in the same industry as the Company.

❏ List of bartering contracts, agreements or arrangements, including a summary of any terms and conditions that the Company is bound to.

Employee-Related Documents

❏ Agreements, contracts or commitments relating to the employment of any person by the Company including:

❏ Nonunion employment agreements

❏ Letters offering employment

❏ Union contracts, memoranda of understanding, side letters, grievance settlement letters

❏ Consulting agreements

❏ Independent Contractor Agreements

❏ Personnel policy manuals and literature relating to all prior, current and proposed programs and benefits

❏ Projections regarding the cost of providing employee health and welfare benefits

❏ Any bonus, deferred compensation, pension, profit sharing, stock option, employee stock purchase, retirement, health and welfare, or other employee benefit plan either maintained by or contributed to by the Company or by any member of the Company's control group of corporations or businesses and covering either current employees or retirees or both, including:

❏ Plan documents and trust and administrative agreements relating to all plans

❏ Current and past summary plan descriptions and all other documents provided to employees regarding the plans

❏ Financial statements of each plan and related audit reports

❏ Current list of all plan assets and related valuations

- ❏ A schedule describing all unfunded pension and related liabilities under any pension or other employee benefit plan
- ❏ Actuarial reports for each defined benefit pension plan
- ❏ Tax returns, reports, determination letters, and other communications or filings with all appropriate taxing authorities (such as the Internal Revenue Service, the Department of Labor, and the Pension Benefit Guaranty Corporation [including Forms 5500, Annual Return/Report of Employee Benefit Plan]).

Real Property

- ❏ Description of real property leased to or by the Company; copies of any leases of real property to or by the Company or any real property options granted to or by the Company.
- ❏ Mortgages to which the Company are a party, or which cover property leased by the Company.
- ❏ Deeds to all real estate owned in whole or in part by the Company, copies of title reports, title policies, surveys, and certifications of occupancy relating thereto.
- ❏ Various or special use permits governing real property occupied by the Company.

Environmental Matters

- ❏ Any information with respect to compliance with federal and state environmental protection laws and regulations, including copies of all environmental permits, approvals, licenses, notices, and registrations necessary for the operation of the Company's business.
- ❏ Information with respect to claims under environmental protection laws and regulations and any notices of violation with respect thereto.
- ❏ Information with respect to inspections, citations, and outstanding enforcement actions involving the Company.
- ❏ Correspondence to and from environmental regulatory authorities relating to any environmental regulatory program.
- ❏ Environmental or safety audits (including employee health and safety audits) and inspection reports, whether performed by the Company, governmental agencies, or any other person.
- ❏ Environmental or safety permit applications currently pending or pending at any time during the last five years, and all related memoranda and correspondence.

❏ All spill reports and notifications.
❏ Intra-company correspondence, including memoranda and reports of
   the Company relating to environmental matters.
❏ Financial estimates and reserves relating to environmental liabilities,
   contingent or otherwise.
❏ Reports of remedial investigations, feasibility studies, or corrective ac-
   tion programs related to environmental matters.
❏ A list of all present and underground, on-ground, and above-ground
   tanks, what they held or hold and where they were or are located.
❏ Schematic diagrams of the Company's facilities, if available.
❏ Information regarding the history of real property owned by the Company prior to acquisition by the Company.

Intellectual Property

❏ All unexpired or expired patents issued to the Company.
❏ Patent applications.
❏ Invention disclosures for which patent applications may be contem-
   plated but have not yet been filed.
❏ A written description or list of important unpatented know-how.
❏ Forms of employee agreements and other procedures used to control
   the ownership, acquisition, security, and confidentiality of information.
❏ Forms of noncompetition agreements used by the Company with a list
   of persons executing each.
❏ "Confidentiality Agreements" executed or received by the Company
   from third parties.
❏ Actual or pending trademark applications, registrations and renewals,
   as well as unregistered trademarks.
❏ A list of each trade name used by the Company, with a description of
   the manner and territory of use, and the states in which fictitious busi-
   ness name filings have been made.
❏ A list of all concurrent use registrations, registration of use of the same
   or similar marks by others, and settlement agreements known to the
   Company.
❏ A description of quality control procedures used by the Company in
   administering any trademark licenses in which it is licensor.
❏ A copy of each copyright application, registration, and renewal.
❏ A copy of each assignment of copyright, including any record of recor-
   dation in the Copyright Office.

❏ A copy of each license of copyright.

❏ A list of disputes, assertions of purported rights, and legal proceedings including those in federal, state, and foreign courts or agencies such as patent, copyright, or trademark offices involving intellectual property ("IP") claims by or against the Company, showing the nature and status of each.

❏ A list of all potential infringement, or other violation of third party IP, known to the Company.

❏ A list of all infringement, known to the Company, of the Company's IP.

❏ A list of all judgments, decrees, other orders of courts or agencies, or agreements or understandings that restrict the Company in their IP rights.

Banking

❏ Bank accounts and signatories.

❏ Bank credit agreements and any other debt instruments and lines of credit.

Litigation/Disputes

❏ A list of, and documents relating to, all litigation, administrative proceedings or governmental investigations or inquiries, pending or threatened.

❏ A list of, and documents relating to, all actual or threatened disputes or grievances of employees pursuant to any union contract.

❏ Consent decrees, judgments, other decrees or orders, settlement agreements, and other agreements to which the Company is a party or is bound, requiring or prohibiting any future activities.

Miscellaneous

❏ Analyses of the Company prepared during the last three years by investment bankers, engineers, management consultants, accountants, or others, including marketing studies, credit reports, and other types of reports, financial or otherwise.

❏ List of all powers of attorney issued and not cancelled.

❏ Organizational charts, and list of all nonunion personnel, listing job titles, descriptions, salaries, start dates, and bonuses paid for the last five years.

❏ List of all internal management reports routinely generated.

TOOL KIT

ROAD MAP FOR TAPPING INTO THE INVESTMENT WORLD

I. Assemble the requisite Tool Kit
   - Develop your elevator pitch.
   - Learn the investment lingo and jargon. If you review the Term Sheet included on page 198, you will see a whole new language. . . the language of investment and deal making.
   - Write a clear and compelling Executive Summary and Business Plan.
   - Develop a clear and cogent Power Point presentation.
   - Build a relevant and networked advisory board; not just 'brand names' who will not roll up their sleeves. This will take time.
   - Research the names of angel investors, angel groups, and the VCs you wish to target. Understand the focus of their investments, their general criteria, and if your company is appropriate for their consideration. All VC firms have excellent Web sites which list their strategy, investment criteria and the companies they have invested in.
   - Construct your "dream team" of potential investors.
   - Work with your advisors to develop a game plan to approach them. Only do this when your company is ready.

II. You are ready to walk in the door
   - Investors want to see your passion, enthusiasm, commitment and willingness to sacrifice for the business.
   - Oftentimes, the decision boils down to personal chemistry, so make sure to be yourself.
   - Emphasize the clear market problem you are solving or the need you will fill.
   - Focus on your customer needs above product design and features.
   - Discuss how you will build a world class team and how they will be rewarded.

III. Here are some common mistakes
   - Walking in the door with no general understanding of the funding process and terminology.
   - Not knowing with whom you will be meeting, or if they are the appropriate person.
   - Your business will not grow to be big enough to be considered for investment.

- An unrealistic business model, revenue model or faulty assumptions. Make sure your basic assumptions are logical and doable.
- Business idea and presentation are not concise — too broad or scattered.
- Not replying to specific questions directly and fully.
- Coming off as not fully honest; obfuscating or being less than candid.
- Not knowing how much money you need to raise, hedging on the amount or not being clear how you intend to spend the capital.
- Failure to listen to investors and market feedback on the terms of your deal: pricing, valuation, the amount of money you are looking to raise.
- Focusing so much on raising money, you neglect to run the business.

CHAPTER 7

SAMPLE ADVISORY AGREEMENT

Date
Name
Address
City, State
Re: Invitation to Join Advisory Board

Dear _____ :

It is with great pleasure that I am writing to officially offer to you a position on the Advisory Board (the *"Advisory Board"*) of "X" Inc. (the *"Company"*). Advisory Board members are expected from time to time to attend meetings of the Advisory Board either in person or by telephone. In addition, Advisory Board members will be expected to provide very limited consulting services, which may consist of drawing upon a member's technical knowledge, management skills, or relationships in either the investment community or potential/existing customer base. If the Company and the member mutually agree, the member may be asked to provide more substantial consulting services. Under these circumstances, the parties shall mutually agree as to any additional compensation to be paid to the member.

As promised, for agreeing to serve on our Advisory Board, the Company will issue to you an option to purchase up to X *shares* of the Common Stock of the Company. The per share exercise price for the option will be $.X. The option will have a term of ten (10) years and will vest in equal quarterly installments. The first installment will be *month, date, year* and the balance in equal, remaining quarterly installments will commence with the quarter starting *month, date, year.* Please understand that your status as an Advisory Board member is "at will," and may be terminated by you or the Company at any time, with or without cause or advance notice. (See note below.)

In consideration of your appointment, you will be required to sign the Company's standard Confidentiality Agreement. The Company also requests notification of your subsequent acceptance of any employment or board membership with any competitor of the Company. I have enclosed the Company's Confidentiality Agreement with this letter.

If you agree to accept a position on the Advisory Board, kindly sign a copy of this letter in the space provided below and return it to me, along with a signed copy of the enclosed Confidentiality Agreement, at your earliest convenience.

I am very excited, (prospective board member's name), about your future affiliation with the Company, and am enthusiastically looking forward to your participation in our growth and success. If you have any questions, please don't hesitate to call me.

Very truly yours,

AGREED TO AND ACCEPTED

By:_____   By:_____
              Name   Name
              Advisor   President & CEO

This _____ day of July, 2002

(Note: In the beginning stages of your company's development, you will have many advisors helping you on an informal basis. They will not expect compensation for their services. After the relationship has solidified, it is then appropriate to formulate such an arrangement and to offer options to the advisors in return for their time and expertise. This would be especially true if you have raised outside capital.)

CHAPTER 8

PROCESS AND SYSTEMS REVIEW

Leadership requires a disciplined approach to conducting business. Former President Harry S. Truman made famous the sign on his desk: "The buck stops here." So now that you are no longer in a position to focus on the day-to-day, and have given up broad decisionmaking authority, it remains your ultimate responsibility as CEO to ensure that the company functions effectively and, of course, within the letter of the law. Appropriate controls are essential.

Based on our interview with Irene Cohen of Flexcorp, we compiled a list of functions and responsibilities for the CEO to review. These systems and controls must be in place in order for the company to grow as seamlessly as possible.

ACCOUNTING SYSTEMS

- Know your expenses
- Make sure you are tracking cash inflows relative to cash outflows
- Know your break-even point and how you are going to reach it
- Set profitability goals for the business overall and individual operating units
- Develop/refine short-term and long-term operating budgets
- Develop/refine forecasts so that you and your team can plan effectively for the future
- Have strong reporting systems in place, both for inside use and for your investors
- Assign areas of accountability for these key functions

HUMAN RESOURCES AND EMPLOYMENT

Make sure you are covered and up-to-date on the current legal and tax status of these issues as well as standards in your industry:

- Payroll taxes
- Pension
- Health benefits
- Employment of foreign nationals
- Sick time and vacation policies
- Formal compensation structure

- Independent contractors
- Incentive stock option and other plans
- Hiring and training
- What functions can/should be outsourced? What is best done in-house?

PROFESSIONAL SERVICE PROVIDERS

Review all relationships; always hire the best:

- Legal
- Accounting
- Tax and finance
- Review all insurance coverage and policies for your firm
- Look for areas to bundle to obtain best prices; for example, insurance

TECHNOLOGY

- Review all software and hardware needs
- Develop a technology plan
- Don't perform noncritical functions in-house if they can be outsourced (see Tool Kit on pages 222–227 for more detail on outsourcing.) But, proceed cautiously on outsourcing technology functions; if you do outsource, make sure there is a key point person inside your company who works closely with your provider and is accountable
- If you depend on proprietary software for your business, make sure to keep control of your source code
- Review technology service providers
- Review hosting providers
- Now that your business has grown, consider bundling services to get better rates
- If you haven't done so before, or haven't updated it in a while, undertake a technology audit
- Review your intellectual property issues

CHAPTER 9

OUTSOURCING OVERVIEW

All businesses, large and small, start-up and established, use outsourcing in many forms to ensure efficiency, and to lower overhead. Even Microsoft, the largest software company in the world, outsources its "Help Desk" function to an outside firm. If outsourcing is good enough for Microsoft, it is definitely something worth considering for your company.

Outsourcing is typically done across broad functional areas. The most common areas as candidates for outsourcing are human resources, accounting, and information technology.

There are no hard-and-fast rules regarding when or what to outsource. But make sure you define your needs up front and what you are looking for. Don't be "sold" something. Know your requirements, interview several providers, and check references.

- Use outsourcing as a means to allow you to focus on your core competencies. If you are a heavily marketing-driven company, by all means consider outsourcing your IT functions. If you are dependent on technology as a vehicle to deliver your product, you may not want to outsource the whole piece. In most companies, things such as Web design and hosting are typically outsourced.
- You may not necessarily save money by outsourcing, but you may find these functional areas run more efficiently.
- Explore full versus partial solutions.
- Human resource outsourcing comes in different forms. Understand the differences in the services offered, along with accountability and liability issues.
- Regarding IT, it is expensive to get the latest in leading-edge technologies. Do not buy into the latest and greatest for technology sake alone. In more than 80 percent of cases, "legacy systems" (the existing IT infrastructure in place) is adequate.
- Outsourcing straightforward functions like accounting and payroll are among the easiest to implement and are highly recommended for small early-stage companies. This function can be overseen by you or your bookkeeper, or CFO, depending on your stage of development. It is much more tricky to outsource sophisticated IT operations. It is easy to abdicate the management of

outsourced talent, and unless someone in-house is held account-
able, serious problems can arise and important services disrupted.
Proceed with caution.
* You still need to direct and manage your outsourced functions.

As always, use your ever-expanding network to source recommenda-
tions for the best providers. The following two Tool Kit items are from a
technology service provider and go into more detail. These address the
outsourcing of IT (Information Technology) functions.

VALUE OF OUTSOURCING

Overview

As competitive pressures and customer and shareholder expectations
continue to increase, the value of outsourcing is likely to steadily rise, as
well. Many companies presently outsourcing various business functions
are actively searching for additional outsourcing opportunities in other
areas.

On the IT front, that trend will translate into additional reliance on
complete, integrated service solutions that are carefully tailored to the
specific requirements and business objectives of various technology customer segments. Whether a company is motivated by speeding time to
market, decreasing investment in infrastructures, making service and/or
subcontractor management more effective, or enhancing their corporate
and product brand, an expert technology support provider should help
stretch their capital and improve customer service, both internally and
externally.

Key Considerations

* Weighing outsourcing pros and cons
* Focus on core competencies
* Making the right business decision

The Value of Direct Support

For those companies looking to enhance direct support for their employees and customers, there is a series of ways that a provider can add value
to the service equation.

Focus on core capabilities. Leveraging a provider's infrastructures and proven processes for service and support, clients can focus on core capabilities and concentrate corporate resources on product development, marketing, sales, and operations.

Avoid service infrastructure investments and planning. With provider's personnel, systems and fixed assets, companies can grow their businesses more quickly without the planning and investment that's often needed in personnel resources, support systems, and capital assets to scale their infrastructure for quality service and support delivery.

Enhance product brand. Providing top-shelf service offerings through an outsourcer with a reputation for quality services delivery enhances a client's product brand.

Eliminate competitive conflicts of interest. Independent service providers that focus solely on support and infrastructure services for the technology industry provide a product agnostic view, help eliminate possible competitive threats, and may reduce revenues to competitors.

Manage service subcontractors effectively. Using outsourcers as the single point of contact of all technology-based infrastructure services minimizes time, effort, and cost of managing multiple services subcontractors and ensures that quality services are delivered to a client's customers.

Preserve investment of technology inventory. Employing outsourcers that offer service options designed to extend the useful life of technology and reduce the need for investment in new equipment purchases can lengthen a system's lifetime and maintain a high level of service.

Speed to deploy technology solutions. Augmenting a client's IT organization with selective skills or technicians in remote locations, technology solutions are implemented faster.

Manage the IT skills shortage by augmenting internal IT staff. Contracting for service delivery instead of investing in personnel for a support function can provide cost-effective coverage.

Expanding Service Portfolios

Outsourcing not only benefits internal technology operations; it can also provide real revenue-building opportunities for companies that resell services.

- Expand revenue through new service offerings
- Lower cost of sales through service packages

- Enhance product brand
- Offer quality corporate service offerings

IT — Most Popular Outsourced Function

Companies that outsource IT are:
- Channel
- Communications
- Service aggregators
- Commercial and government

Reasons for outsourcing across all companies are:
- A need for direct technology support for employees or customers.
- A desire to expand their service portfolio through an outsourcing partnership that enables them to offer additional technology services to their customers.

(Courtesy of Cody Traver, CEO, CIO Global, www.cioglobal.com)

AVOIDING THE PITFALLS OF IT OUTSOURCING

Overview
Companies may be in trouble without a carefully thought-out service level agreement (SLA). One of the most common mistakes made when outsourcing is an incomplete (or absent entirely) SLA.

The greatest pitfall is the lack of oversight and preparation. Set the tone for success before the outsourcing arrangement begins. Internal or externally obtained expertise in vendor selection and management will aid you in finding and securing the right vendor.

Musts
- Analyze your company's communication needs
- Develop an RFP (Request for Proposals) consistent with your goals
- Select business-oriented vendor candidates
- Manage the bidders' process
- Manage vendor inquiries during the RFP process
- Review, evaluate, and rank the proposals
- Package your evaluation into a concise report

- Guide your selection of the best vendor for your business
- Support your procurement staff
- Oversee service commencement

Common Mistakes

- Failure to acknowledge your organization's values and assumptions
- Underestimating what it takes to produce a good RFP
- Resisting the effort of developing an RFP, or short-circuiting with an inadequate set of "requirements"
- Assuming that new technology is cheaper than and as reliable as older technology
- Assuming that, following industry spending guidelines, IT "best practices" ensures the best outcome from the IT department

Network Project Failures

Outsourcing project failures come under two general headings from user perspectives:

1. Technical failures (more common since the early 1990s)
2. Justification failures (a huge increase in occurrence)
   - Both types of failure stem from a few common blunders
   - Failure to differentiate between network operations and support organizations, resulting in false cost assumptions and economic failure
   - Support organizations are event driven, resulting in a tactical operations mindset that is anathema to strategic planning
   - Retention of skilled network operations staff because of misuse on non-challenging tasks, resulting in management displeasure and staff dissatisfaction

The Art of Outsourcing—Avoiding the Pitfalls

Preparation is the key to success.

- Ensure that applications, desktop systems, and routine user support are all covered. Consolidate functions of a dual-role staff. Thirty percent possible cost savings.
- Accurately determine components of network costs; e.g., capital costs, monthly service costs, and personnel costs.

- Be certain of the validity of predicted savings; i.e., be sure that any staff reduction impact is covered by the outsourcing vendor.
- Consider the cost of interaction with the outsourcing provider and develop a well defined service level agreement.

(Courtesy of Cody Traver, CEO, CIO Global, www.cioglobal.com)

PERSONAL DEVELOPMENT PLAN

In reading this book and working through the Toolkit, no doubt you have identified a number of ways to improve your company's performance. The purpose of this exercise is to enable you to develop a specific plan to implement at least two changes to that end.

Such changes may be personal, like improving your influence skills or handling criticism more effectively. Others may be organizational, like restructuring around customers or modifying rewards systems to reinforce greater collaboration among your employees.

To create your personal development plan, complete the planning guide that follows.

Planning Guide

Choose one or two areas you think would benefit most from increased, sustained attention. After selecting these target areas and noting them below, list measures of success beside them; that is, how will you know if you have succeeded in meeting your improvement targets. Then, develop plans for improving your performance, using the following pages.

	Target Areas	*Measure of Success*
1.	_____	_____
2.	_____	_____

PLAN FOR TARGET 1

Steps for Performance Improvement
Steps   List the steps required to improve your performance in Target 1, the deadlines by which you want to accomplish these steps, obstacles that might prevent you from improving, and your plans for overcoming those obstacles.

Steps	Deadlines	Obstacles	Plans

Assistance
People/Relationships   List the people with whom you will need to work to achieve your performance-improvement objectives including their relationship to you. Note the type of help you will need, and your deadline for obtaining it.

People/Relationship	Specific Help Needed	Deadlines

PLAN FOR TARGET 2

Steps for Performance Improvement
Steps   List the steps required to improve your performance in Target 2, the deadlines by which you want to accomplish these steps, obstacles that might prevent you from improving, and your plans for overcoming those obstacles.

Steps	Deadlines	Obstacles	Plans

Assistance
People/Relationships   List the people with whom you will need to work to achieve your performance-improvement objectives including their relationship to you. Note the type of help you will need, and your deadline for obtaining it.

People/Relationship	Specific Help Needed	Deadlines

The Personal Development Plan is produced courtesy of The Whiteley Group

TOOL KIT

RESOURCE GUIDE

There is a wealth of resources available to entrepreneurs—books, online services, the Web sites of major accounting firms, local Chambers of Commerce, and business development centers. These are just some of our favorites:

For Basic Business Advice for Entrepreneurs:

- www.inc.com (*Inc. Magazine*'s Web site)
- www.sba.gov (Web site of the Small Business Administration)
- See also the SBA Women's Business Center at www.onlinewbc.gov
- Startup.Wsj.com (*Start Up Journal,* the *Wall Street Journal*'s Center for Entrepreneurship)
- www.entreworld.org (Kauffmann Center for Entrepreneurial Leadership)
- www.asbdc-us.org (Association for Small Business Development Centers)
- www.Technologyventuretoolbox.com (Technology Venture Toolbox, comprehensive advice on startup issues)
- www.bplans.com (business plans online)

Other Business Plans and Planning Tools

- www.pasware.com (business forms and related information)
- www.mitenterpriseforum.org (MIT Enterprise Forum; helpful information and links to other sources)

For Researching Legal Issues

(Please note that we recommend that you engage a top-notch law firm.)

- www.gigalaw.com
- www.nolo.com

For Human Resource Planning

- www.shrm.org (Society for Human Resource Management)
- www.humanresources.org (National Human Resources)

Other Helpful Organizations

- www.uschamber.com (U.S. Chamber of Commerce)
- www.score.org (Service Corps of Retired Executives)
- www.wbenc.org (WBENC-Women's Business Enterprise National Council)

Women's Business Organizations

Center for Women's Business Research (www.cwbr.org)
National Association of Women Business Owners
World WIT (Women in Technology: www.worldwit.org)
WEST (Women Entrepreneurs in Science and Technology: www.westorg.org)
WE Inc. (Women Entrepreneurs Inc: www.we-inc.org)
www.women-21.gov (helpful site to access resources provided by the federal government)

Most major cities have business assistance programs, local universities, or community college business development centers. Many have organizations devoted to women entrepreneurs such as the Center for Women and Enterprise (www.cweboston.org) in Boston.

For Raising Money

- Springboard Venture Capital Forums for Women (www.springboardenterprises.org)
- Forum for Women Entrepreneurs (www.few.org)
- Technology Capital Network at MIT (www.tcnmit.org) has an Internet-based service that matches entrepreneurs with investors.

MEET THE ENTREPRENEURS

This book would not be complete without the invaluable contributions of the entrepreneurs featured throughout our chapters. Our boundless thanks to each and every one for their time, candor, and courage in sharing their inspirational and instructive stories. If you are interested in learning more about these remarkable women and their companies—or even in becoming a customer—we have provided relevant contact information below. Tell 'em 8Wings sent you!

Chapter 2: Passion

Cheryl Straughter
Owner
Keith's Place
469 Blue Hill Avenue
Boston, Massachusetts 02121
e-mail: Keithsplace02121@aol.com

Maxine Clark
Chief Executive Bear
Build-A-Bear Workshop®
1954 Innerbelt Business Center Dr.
St. Louis, Missouri 63114-5760
e-mail: maxine@buildabear.com
www.buildabear.com

Jaimee Wolf
Chief Executive Officer
Xicat Interactive, Inc.
800 East Broward Boulevard, Suite 700
Fort Lauderdale, Florida 33301
e-mail: jbwolf@xicat.com
www.xicat.com

Marcia Wieder
Marcia Wieder Enterprises
110 Pacific Avenue #355
San Francisco, California 94111
e-mail: mw@marciaw.com
www.marciaw.com

Chapter 3: Vision

Selima Salaun
Selima Optique
899 Madison Avenue (one of many retail locations in New York)
New York, New York
www.selimaoptique.com

Eva Jeanbart-Lorenzotti
Chief Executive Officer
Vivre
11 East 26th Street
New York, New York 10010
e-mail: customercare@vivre.com
www.vivre.com

Maria Cirino, CEO
Guardent, Inc.
75 Third Avenue
Waltham, Massachusetts 02451

Jenny Cohen
Chief Executive Officer
Songmasters
110 W. 96th Street
New York, New York 10025
e-mail: jennifer.cohen@songmasters.com

Chapter 4: Pioneering Spirit

Sharon P. Whiteley
President and Chief Executive Officer
ThirdAge Inc.

210 Lincoln Street, Suite 302
Boston, MA 02111
e-mail: sharon@whitecomp.com
www.thirdage.com

Cynthia Fisher
Chief Executive Officer
BioMed 20/20 Technologies, Inc.
275 Grove Street, Building 2, 4th Floor
Auburndale, Massachusetts 02466
e-mail: ddowning@biomed2020.com
www.biomed2020.com

Chapter 5: Tenacity

Robin Chase
Chairman
Zipcar
675 Massachusetts Avenue, 9th Floor
Cambridge, Massachusetts 02139
e-mail: info@zipcar.com
www.zipcar.com

Judy George
Chief Executive Officer
Domain
51 Morgan Drive
Norwood, Massachusetts 02062
e-mail: Jgeorge@domain-home.com
www.domain-home.com

Sheila Schectman
Chief Executive Officer
Giftcorp
20–28 Sargeant Street
Hartford, Connecticut 06105
e-mail: Sheila@giftcorp.com
www.giftcorp.com

Chapter 6: Raising Capital

Janet Kraus
Chief Executive Officer
Circles
300 Congress Street
Boston, Massachusetts 02110
e-mail: requests@circles.com
www.circles.com

Patricia Meisner
President and Chief Executive Officer
Red Tail Solutions
171 Main Street, Suite 210
Milford, MA 01751
e-mail: pmeisner@advance-com.net
www.advancecom.net

Chapter 7: Focus, Feedback, and Flexibility

Antoinette Bruno
Chief Executive Officer
StarChefs
9 East 19th Street, 19th Floor
New York, New York 10003
e-mail: bruno@starchefs.com
www.starchefs.com

Paula White
600 lb gorillas
20 Arrowhead Road
Wrentham, Massachusetts 02093
doughballs@aol.com

Patricia Pomerlau
Chief Executive Officer
CEOExpress Company
470 Atlantic Avenue
Boston, Massachusetts 02110
e-mail: patpom@ceoexpress.com
www.ceoexpress.com

Chapter 8. Leadership Lessons

Tena Clark
DiscMarketing
35 West Dayton Street
Pasadena, California 91105
e-mail: tena@discmarketing.com
www.discmarketing.com

Lori Schafer
President and Chief Executive Officer
Marketmax, Inc.
14 Audobon Road
Wakefield, Massachusetts 01880
e-mail: info@marketmax.com
www.marketmax.com

Lore Harp McGovern
Private Investor
lore@LoreHarpMcGovern.com

Chapter 9. Life After the Survival Stage

Irene Cohen
Chief Executive Officer
FlexCorp Systems
330 Madison Avenue
New York, New York 10017
e-mail: irenecohen@aol.com
www.flexcorpsys.com

Carolee Friedlander
President and Chief Executive Officer
Carolee Designs, Inc.
19 East Elm Street
Greenwich, Connecticut 06830
e-mail: Carolee@carolee.com
www.carolee.com

Rhona Silver
Chief Executive Officer
The New Huntington Townhouse

124 East Jericho Turnpike
Huntington Station, New York 11746
e-mail: info@newhuntingtontownhouse.com
www.newhuntingtontownhouse.com

Barbara Corcoran
e-mail: barbara@corcoran.com

. . . .

Special thanks to:

Diane Darling
Effective Networking
e-mail: diane@EffectiveNetworking.com

Jill Card
IBEX Process Technologies
www.ibexprocess.com

Cody Traver
CIO Global
www.cioglobal.com

INDEX